P-40 WARHAWK

Frederick A. Johnsen

MBI Publishing Company

Dedication

For Sharon Lea

First published in 1998 by MBI Publishing Company, 729 Prospect Avenue, PO Box 1, Osceola, WI 54020-0001 USA

© Frederick A. Johnsen, 1998

All rights reserved. With the exception of quoting brief passages for the purposes of review, no part of this publication may be reproduced without prior written permission from the Publisher.

The information in this book is true and complete to the best of our knowledge. All recommendations are made without any guarantee on the part of the author or Publisher, who also disclaim any liability incurred in connection with the use of this data or specific details.

We recognize that some words, model names, and designations, for example, mentioned herein are the property of the trademark holder. We use them for identification purposes only. This is not an official publication.

MBI Publishing Company books are also available at discounts in bulk quantity for industrial or sales-promotional use. For details write to Special Sales Manager at Motorbooks International Wholesalers & Distributors, 729 Prospect Avenue, PO Box 1, Osceola, WI 54020-0001 USA.

Library of Congress Cataloging-in-Publication Data
Johnsen, Frederick A.
p. cm.—(Warbird history)
Includes index.
ISBN 0-7603-0253-7 (pbk. : alk. paper)
1. P-40 (Fighter planes)—History. 2. World War, 1939-1945—Aerial operations. I. Title. II. Series: warbird history.
UG1242.F5J6324 1998
623.7'464—dc21 98-23724

On the front cover: An impeccable P-40E, sporting a ferocious sharkmouth, carries the markings of the Second Pursuit Squadron of the American Volunteer Group—better known as the Flying Tigers. P-40Es like this one were capable of 354 mph at 15,000 feet, and had a service ceiling of 29,000 feet. *John M. Dibbs*

On the back cover, top: The third configuration for the XP-40 radiator set the standard for early production models. *Curtiss Wright via Peter M. Bowers collection*

On the back cover, bottom: Air rushing around the contours of the fuselage directed the exhaust in a pattern caught in this photo of a P-40E, representative of new models available at the time of the attack on Pearl Harbor. *Peter M. Bowers collection*

Printed in the United States of America

Contents

Preface

It is impossible to conjure the visage of a Curtiss P-40 without thinking of heroism. The P-40, elderly even as World War II began, was the vehicle that was available when retired Captain Claire Chennault and his American Volunteer Group—the famous Flying Tigers—needed it to help China battle the Japanese. As the Flying Tigers earned a well-deserved measure of honor over China and Burma in late 1941 and early 1942, they also added momentum to the ultimate characterization of the P-40 as a sharkmouth-emblazoned, snarling warbird possessing remarkable strength. No matter that others used the sharkmouth device; it is forever seared in history as the sign of the Flying Tigers.

Fighting in the Aleutian Island chain pitted P-40 pilots against the Japanese—and the weather. The invasion of North Africa included seemingly incongruous launches of Army Air Forces P-40s from Navy aircraft carriers. Later, the first black aviators to wear Army Air Forces uniforms would learn to fly fighters by climbing into the cockpits of Curtiss P-40 Warhawks.

From aerial combat to a second career as a ground attack aircraft, P-40s served throughout the war. If they were bested in some performance areas by enemy and Allied aircraft, P-40s had a simple sturdiness that still found utility in an Allied war effort stretched around the globe.

Wartime documents help bring the P-40 story to life with an authenticity that sometimes transcends current political correctness. So don't be shocked at the occasional use of wartime slang in vintage sources in this book. The terminology either had no offensive connotation back then, or else it very deliberately did in the heat of battle. Let it be what it is—the flavor of World War II, more than a half century old.

The presentation of this P-40 history owes a lot to the unsung Army Air Forces cameramen who preserved Warhawk images on film in often-rustic field conditions. Much of the documentation cited in this narrative was made available by the helpful staff at the Air Force Historical Research Agency at Maxwell Air Force Base, Alabama, where the public may buy microfilmed histories of Air Force units that did so much to win World War II. Other individuals and organizations who helped include: Major General John R. Alison, USAF (Retired), Gene Chase, Jeff Ethell, Tom Foote, Ken Glassburn, Ben Howser, Don Keller (Air Depot, Beaverton, Oregon), Dr. Gary Leiser, Fred LePage, Dave Menard, Garry Pape, Dave and Jeff Sturges (Columbia Airmotive, Troutdale, Oregon), and Bob Wilson (12th Bomb Group Association).

Ace fighter–writer Barrett Tillman graciously obliged by occasionally looking over my shoulder at sections of this manuscript. And the P-40 never had a better friend than Wayne Fiamengo, who has made the Tomahawk and Warhawk his objects of study for more than the three decades I have known him. Special thanks for sharing your information, Wayne.

From the late 1960s through the decade of the 1970s, as I photographed aviation events in the United States and Canada, I was mentored by the best air-to-air photographer in the business: Jim Larsen. For this book, Jim graciously lent some of his outstanding photos of warbird P-40s.

Some photo credits in this volume are abbreviated SDAM, for San Diego Aerospace Museum. Thanks to Ray Wagner and the staff of that museum's archives for their wonderful assistance.

And kudos to Michael Haenggi, my editor, for giving positive direction to projects under his stewardship at MBI Publishing Company.

Frederick A. Johnsen

P-40 Lineage

Curtiss engineer Donovan Berlin spearheaded the project to install a streamlined, liquid-cooled Allison V-1710 engine in the airframe of the 10th production P-36A Hawk, replacing the Hawk's stocky radial R-1830 powerplant. Calling the result XP-40, Curtiss flew the aircraft on 14 October 1938 and submitted it to the Air Corps for possible production. It was a humble beginning, using a modest existing airframe, yet it would yield one of the signature aircraft of World War II, still widely recognized as an icon of that era.

The XP-40 was attractive on several counts. The new Curtiss fighter embraced the inline Allison engine then finding favor in the Air Corps. (Only the Republic P-47 would emerge as a serious Army Air Forces day fighter powered by an air-cooled engine during World War II.) The XP-40 represented a relatively easy segue from the P-36 already in production, using, at least initially, much of the same airframe with modifications, instead of designing and building an all-new structure.

The P-40 and many fighters of the era were sent to the National Advisory Committee for Aeronautics (NACA) for drag testing in the NACA's full-scale wind tunnel at Langley, Virginia. The cleanup work done to the P-40 airframe in the NACA tunnel promised to raise its top speed by 30 miles per hour. Though not all NACA recommendations for aircraft clean-ups were feasible for production and operational use, the NACA's engineers did contribute to the efficiency and performance of the P-40[1] and many other World War II aircraft.

Ironically, the first aircraft to be tested for drag cleanup in the NACA full-scale tunnel was the Brewster F2A Buffalo, a Naval fighter that would remain less than stellar in brief U.S. combat use, but which gained 31 miles per hour once NACA engineers applied all their talents to its airframe in April of 1938. News spread about the Buffalo's metamorphosis, and soon the Army and Navy were queuing up to test new designs at Langley for aerodynamic efficiency. The first four aircraft tested in this way were Navy projects, followed by

Curtiss designer Donovan Berlin smiled broadly with his successful P-40, the subject of the largest Air Corps contract as of that era. *SDAM*

In its second iteration, the XP-40, serial 38-010, mounted its radiator deep under the chin. Landing-gear fairings were more extensive when the photo was taken than on later P-40s. *Peter M. Bowers collection*

the Curtiss XP-37, P-36A, and the XP-40 in August 1938.[2]

The test routine involved removing and fairing those aspects of an airframe suspected of contributing to drag. The resulting clean airframe, devoid of radio masts and with fuselage openings taped and smoothed over, formed a low-drag baseline. Obviously, such a configuration was not practical for a flying, serviceable aircraft needing radios and other equipment, but the degree of improvement between the original configuration and the streamlined baseline could be quantified, and those streamlining changes that were practical could be applied on the production line.

Following its 1938 cleanup testing at Langley, the XP-40 returned there in March 1939 to become the first of several P-40s studied for a variety of test and evaluation purposes. The XP-40 remained with NACA until March 1944, according to NACA records. Two other P-40s came to Langley in June and July 1940. As combat and design advances came into play, the NACA at Langley ran flight tests on a number of warplanes, including tail tests on P-40s that ultimately resulted in the broader chord of the K-model Warhawk's vertical fin. P-40E number 41-5534 stayed at Langley between March and July 1942, followed by a P-40K-1 from July 1942 to October 1944. Another E-model (42-458010) was tested in 1942 as well as a Merlin-powered F-model (41-13600). The last Warhawk listed by the NACA at Langley was F-model 41-14119.[3]

The role of the NACA in advancing the state of aeronautics for American manufacturers of the era was substantial, and proved very valuable to the war effort. Even after major aircraft drag–reduction programs had taken place, elements of the NACA worked on diverse speed improvement schemes, such as angling exhaust stacks to the rear to utilize exhaust gases for thrust. These features benefited the P-40 and other aircraft.

Curtiss Hits the Jackpot

The XP-40 metamorphosed, starting with its radiator mounted ventrally behind the wing, and gradually moving forward to a chin location for production variants. After testing and comparing the XP-40 with other fighter contenders, the Air Corps made history on 26 April 1939, when it placed its largest order to date for an Air Corps fighter—the contract called for 524 P-40s to be delivered for a price of almost $13 million.[4] This order made the P-40 the first of the new breed of liquid-cooled Air Corps fighters to go into production and service.[5]

Bypassing the normal Y-prefixed service test option, the Air Corps went directly from XP-40 to straight P-40 production aircraft, designated by Curtiss as Model 81. Powered by the V-1710-33 engine, these first production P-40s carried a pair of .50-caliber machine guns in the upper cowling and one .30-caliber weapon in each wing. The P-40 first flew on 4 April 1940, and beginning in June, Curtiss delivered 200 of these initial variants. Sixteen of them were allotted to the Soviet Union. One straight P-40 (serial 40-326) became the sole P-40A in 1942 when it was modified as a photo-reconnaissance aircraft, and another (39-221) was modified to become the P-40G,

For airflow visualization tests, lampblack was allowed to stream from behind the propeller spinner of the XP-40 in its second configuration. *Peter M. Bowers collection*

YP-37 was Curtiss' and the Air Corps' first effort at mating the Allison V-1710 engine to a fighter airframe in 1937. Growing from the P-36, the YP-37 was lengthened and used a far aft cockpit location. The radiator was side-mounted. Less-than-anticipated performance led to the discontinuance of the P-37 in favor of the P-40. *SDAM/Bodie collection*

Curtiss' desire to improve on the broad frontal area of the radial-engine P-36 led to the XP-42 of 1939, with an enclosed R-1830 radial engine and a large chin air scoop. Ultimately, the bullet-nosed Allison-engined P-40 would outlive this experiment. When photographed, the XP-42 had been painted with temporary camouflage. *SDAM*

sometimes called the XP-40G. The P-40B, distinguishable chiefly for the additional .30-caliber machine gun in each wing, began deliveries in January 1941. One hundred thirty-one B-models were built.

The P-40C technically filled the last of the original 524–plane order, with 193 C-models built. Delivered between March and May of 1941, P-40Cs introduced internal leak-proof tanks plus the capability to carry a centerline drop tank, as Curtiss responded to evolving combat dictates then unfolding in Europe.

The use of a centerline bomb shackle on the P-40C to carry a droppable fuel tank was a foray into conflicting doctrinal opinions for the prewar Air Corps. External tanks had been deleted from Air Corps fighters partly under the banner of safety, but also at least in part because some in the service believed shackles that could carry gasoline tanks could be used to carry bombs, and the Air Corps was on guard against having its fighter assets tapped as close air support ground-attack machines coveted by Army ground commanders.[6]

The ultimate expression of this suspicion came to light in the hectic days immediately following the Japanese raid on Pearl Harbor, when P-40 operators in the Philippines urgently requested an explanation about an apparent shortcoming on their P-40s: While the Curtiss fighters could carry a bomb on the centerline shackle, the aircraft had no means to arm the bombs as they dropped. In other words, the shackles had been installed without the ability to use an arming wire that blocked spinning up and arming of a vane-driven fuse until the bomb was released. The lack of this feature, the Air Force explained, was because the shackles had only been approved for installation as gas tank shackles; no bomb-carrying capability had been approved.[7] The necessities of combat would see all major United States Army Air Forces (USAAF) fighters of World War II equipped to carry drop tanks, with bombing as an alternate use. The P-40 would ultimately earn its keep in many theaters of operation as a fighter-bomber long after its capabilities as a dogfighter had been surpassed by other warplanes.

British Tomahawk variants encompassed the evolution from P-40 through P-40C. The Tomahawk I was similar in most respects to the straight P-40, although the British Tomahawk I introduced two machine guns in each wing. These soon became noncombatant aircraft in British use. Three went to Canada. The designation Tomahawk II was applied to other early P-40s, with Tomahawk IIA equating with the P-40B, incorporating externally covered self-sealing gas tanks and some protective armor. Tomahawk IIBs, totaling 930 aircraft, were generally the same as the P-40C.

Curtiss could not have foreseen the prosperity it would enjoy in this early prewar period. Production of Tomahawk variants was so hectic that for a while part of the Curtiss-Wright Kenmore plant employee parking lot at Buffalo, New York, was converted to serve as an auxiliary runway for production flight testing of newly built P-40s. P-40s also were built at Curtiss' North Elmwood factory. Curtiss stole the march on competitors by having, first, a viable production fighter at a time when other American manufacturers were still evolving their designs, and second, manufacturing capacity. Through much of 1942, Curtiss symbolized the fabled Arsenal of Democracy, furnishing P-40s in quantity while other fighters were still coming up to speed. But the boom days of 1940–42, although sustained by ongoing wartime contracts, may have hurt Curtiss in the long run by substituting a bird in the hand for any truly new-generation designs later on.

A defining change in the design of P-40s occurred with the introduction of the P-40D in 1941. Just as the thrust line changed on P-38 Lightnings when newer Allisons with spur reduction gearing were installed, the same evolution began with the P-40D. The 1,150-horsepower V-1710-39 engine put the engine thrust line, and hence the center of the large propeller spinner, almost in line with the exhaust stacks. This led to a more pronounced radiator/oil cooler chin inlet arrangement than on previous P-40s. Atop the cowl, a carburetor air scoop graced the nose. Fuselage guns were deleted, and a total of four .50-caliber machine guns were placed in the wings. A centerline shackle under the wing could accommodate a 52-gallon drop tank or a 500-pound bomb, and attachments on the undersides of the wings could be used to carry six 20-pound bombs. Self-sealing gas tanks and protective armor weighing 175 pounds made the D-models more serious combat contenders.

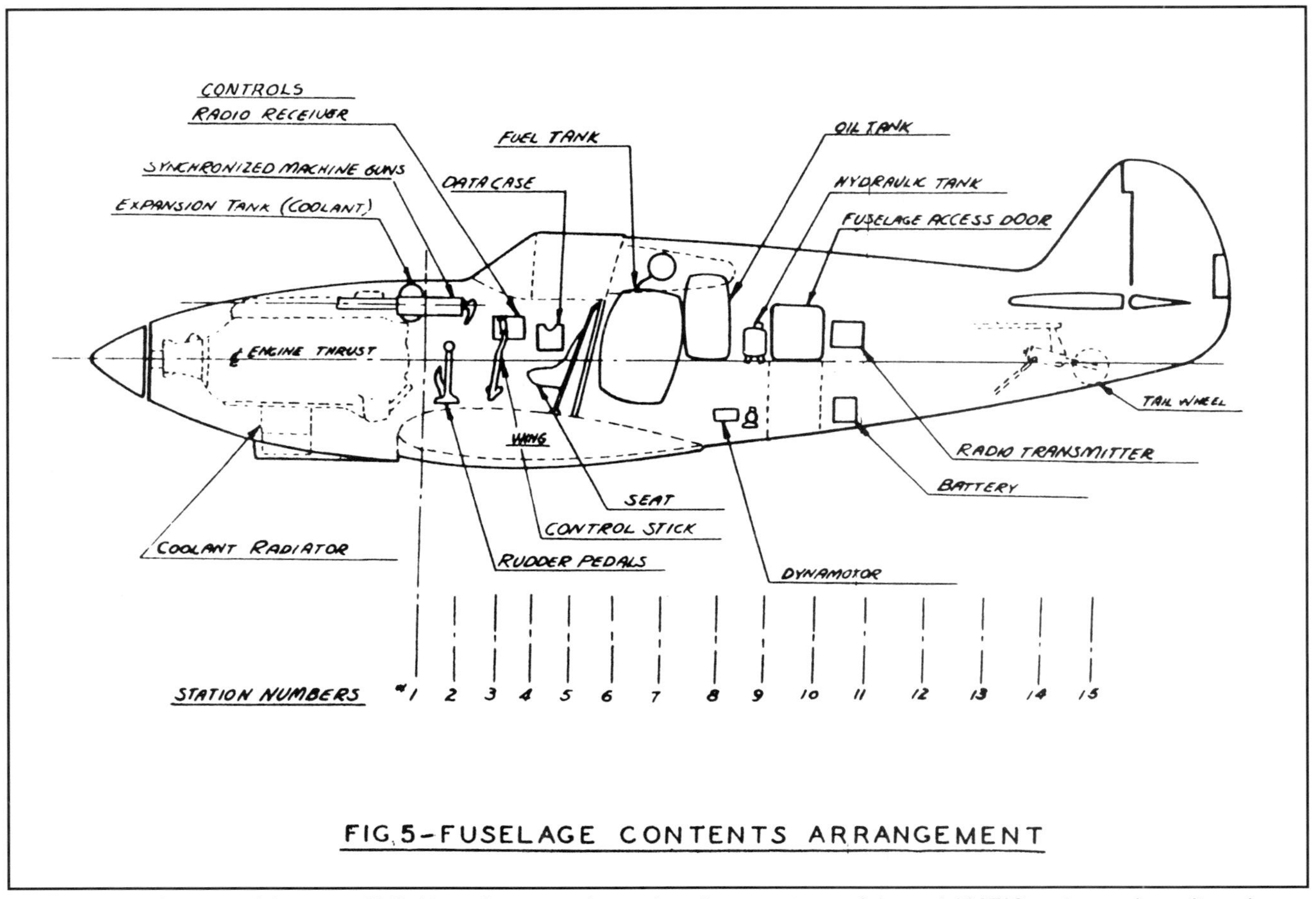

Phantom side elevation of the second XP-40 configuration shows the relative position of the early V-1710 engine to thrust line, plus the arrangement of many items in fuselage. Later addition of spur reduction gear to the Allison engine boosted power and necessitated redesigned nose contours as thrust line was raised. *Courtesy Project Tomahawk*

Though only 23 P-40Ds went to the USAAF, 560 comparable aircraft were taken on by the Royal Air Force (RAF) as the Kittyhawk I.[8]

The P-40E represented the largest P-40 production run of its time, totaling 820 aircraft. The P-40E packed six wing-mounted .50-caliber machine guns and deleted a provision for 20-millimeter wing guns not used in D-models. Added to this were 1,500 P-40E-1s supplied under Lend-Lease to Great Britain, with the suffix -1 noting they were fitted with some British equipment that varied from traditional American P-40Es. In British service, the P-40E-1 was the Kittyhawk IA. Some E-1s remained in USAAF service, and six became Brazilian fighters.

The XP-40F started life as a P-40D (40-360). It mounted a Rolls-Royce Merlin engine and first took flight on 30 June 1941. Performance was encouraging, and 1,311 production F-models were eventually built. A quick recognition feature for Merlin-powered P-40s was the absence of the carburetor scoop on top of the nose cowling, resulting in a smooth line from the propeller spinner back to the windscreen. After 699 P-40Fs were built, the P-40F-5 introduced a 20-inch aft fuselage extension that improved directional stability. As the Kittyhawk II, 150 F-models were earmarked for Great Britain, although some of these wound up in USAAF service.

The designation P-40G was given to 43 straight P-40s, which followed a fellow P-40 modified as the XP-40G by substituting Tomahawk IIA wings carrying four .30-caliber machine guns. In fact, the 16 straight P-40s sent to the Soviet Union beginning in the fall of 1941 were converted to P-40G status.

Cancellation of the P-40H left a gap in the suffixes for the line; the letter "I" was never used, and the proposed P-40J was to have been a turbo-supercharged, Allison-powered variant.

The P-40K resumed Allison engine use and enjoyed a production run of 1,300 aircraft. Essentially an improvement on E-model technology, with V-1710-73 engines delivering better performance at altitude, the P-40Ks started delivery in August 1942. A dorsal fin extension gave the K-models a distinctively broader vertical fin than that of other P-40 models, while counteracting a tendency of the P-40 to swing its tail during takeoff. A later fuselage extension, which was a high-speed control fix, alternately answered this problem, beginning with P-40K-10s.

P-40L was the model designation applied to 700 Merlin-powered P-40s similar to the P-40F-5 except for minor equipment variances. P-40L-5s used only four wing guns; P-40L-10s had electric aileron trim tabs. So similar were the L-models to the P-40F that 100 P-40Ls supplied to Great Britain kept the earlier designation of Kittyhawk II first applied to the British F-models. Some P-40K and later L-models , as well as some P-40Ms, were grouped together by the British as the Kittyhawk III. A side effect of the P-40L was the departure of designer Donovan Berlin from Curtiss, unhappy about changes made by the company to that model, according to publisher Joseph V. Mizrahi. Berlin's departure stripped the company of a bright and driven engineering mind.

The P-40M was close in configuration to the P-40K-20, except the M used an Allison V-1710-81 engine. Starting with P-40M-1s, the ailerons were reinforced; the -5s had improvements to carburetor air filtering, and P-40M-10s used a revised landing gear warning system, as well as an altered fuel system. The British employed the P-40M as the Kittyhawk III; several also went to Brazil.

If the P-40E set the tone for early P-40 traits, the ultimate production changes were embodied during the P-40N's construction run at Curtiss. First off the line, the P-40N-1s had lightened weight, only four guns, no wing bomb racks, manual landing gear and flap operation, and increased armor, all riding behind a V-1710-81 Allison.

With the P-40N-5, Curtiss introduced a cut-down deck behind the pilot's seat, still faired with Plexiglas to a high aft fuselage, as opposed to a bubble canopy. The N-5s returned wing bomb racks to the Warhawk's repertoire and increased fuel capacity again. The N-5s also used 27-inch main wheels; by the time P-40N-40s were built, main wheel size had increased to 30 inches. The P-40N-40s also used metal-clad ailerons. In British service, the P-40N was the Kittyhawk IV. One hundred and thirty went to the Soviet Union, and forty-one equipped the Brazilian air force, some flying in Brazil as late as 1958.[9]

The third straight P-40 (39-158) was photographed in prewar natural metal finish. *Author collection*

The P-40P was to have been a Merlin-engined variant with traits similar to the P-40N-1 and N-5; in fact, that is how these airframes were completed, as N-models with Allison engines.

XP-40Q was applied to a substantially modified Warhawk with a bubble canopy and, ultimately, wing-root coolant radiators that replaced an inboard gun in each wing. A revised chin scoop and, later, squared wingtips further defined the Q-model. A two-stage mechanical supercharger promised improved altitude performance. All the changes let the XP-40Q attain 422 miles per hour at 20,500 feet, earning it the crown as the fastest P-40 model. But this was insufficient to warrant production. Two XP-40Qs were modified from P-40K airframes; a third started life as a P-40N.

P-40R was used to designate a scattering of P-40F and P-40L airframes that received Allison engines instead of their intended Merlins. The R-models were used for training purposes. P-40R-1 defined the F-model conversions; P-40R-2 was used for the former L-models.

TP-40 described several trainer conversions, including dual-control Warhawks intended to make the leap from an AT-6 trainer to a fighter less daunting.

Comparisons With Other Fighters

By December 1940, detailed comparisons had been made in England using an early P-40, a Spitfire Mk. II, and a Hurricane Mk. II. The P-40 was not operationally equipped, but carried a gross test load of 7,240 pounds, while the British fighters carried service loads. Measurements for all three fighters included:[10]

	P-40	Spitfire II	Hurricane II
Gross test load (lbs.)	7,240	6,195	6,886
Wing loading (lbs./sq. ft.)	30.5	25.5	26.7
Maximum speed (mph)	354	365	325
Maximum ceiling (ft.)	32,000	37,600	37,600

A radiogram to the secretary of war described the comparisons and noted, "The P-40 will be further tested when it is equipped for combat. It will carry armor and four caliber .303 free-firing wing and two caliber .50 synchronized machine guns." The notation of four caliber .303 (British terminology) wing guns suggests this test P-40 was equivalent to a Tomahawk I.[11]

The evaluation of the maximum ceiling was telling: Already in 1940, the Merlin-powered Spitfire and Hurricane were more than a mile above the P-40 with its Allison powerplant and less-capable blower. The memo discussed performance of the three fighters, "British test section considers P-40 as maneuverable as British fighters below 20,000 feet but less so at greater heights." A clue to this phenomenon lies in the heavier wing loading of the P-40. (Later in World War II, even B-24 pilots sometimes found they could convert their relatively lighter wing loading, *versus* Me-109s, into a turning contest that would force the higher-loaded wing of the fighter to stall; Cold War B-36 pilots knew the same thing when it came to high-altitude turns in their mammoth bombers against jet fighter contemporaries like the F-86 and MiG-15.)

The comparison memo urged permitting a 300-rpm higher power setting in the P-40 in the hope of achieving about 3,000 additional feet of ceiling and greater maneuverability at altitude. Almost as an aside, the memo reported, "Partially because of the transparent material used in the canopy the visibility in this plane [the P-40] is much superior to that of either the Hurricane or Spitfire."[12]

Trends were evident as early as 1940 that showed the P-40's relative strengths and weaknesses.

A succinct message from one American officer of giant stature to another was a May 1942 memo from General Douglas MacArthur to General Henry "Hap" Arnold regarding early combat evaluations of P-40s pitted against Japanese fighters (identified as "0," for Zero, in the message). MacArthur's memo said: "Below 15,000 feet the P-40 is slightly faster on straight and level flight, and is slower above 15,000 feet. At all altitudes the Jap '0' outclimbs our P-40. . . . The '0' is a circle-combat type of plane, will out maneuver P-40 at any altitude; highly maneuverable and considered superior." But the P-40 "has a decidedly superior firepower and can out dive the '0'." MacArthur noted the P-40 "also can break combat at any time by a rolling dive." Interestingly, at the

The cockpit layout of a P-40B shows cutouts in the instrument panel to accommodate receivers of nose-mounted guns (not installed in photo). Wing guns were charged by pulling charging handles mounted in the center, below the instrument panel. In the photo, four handles are installed, suggesting the configuration of a P-40C rather than B as listed on the original photo. This may have been a test aircraft subject to modification. *Peter M. Bowers collection*

early stage in the war when the memo was written, MacArthur said different pilots opined that the Bell P-39 Airacobra, which had been in combat less than a month, was 5 to 20 percent better than the P-40 in combat with the "0." [13] (Later in the year when P-40s were able to engage Japanese formations at altitudes where early P-39s struggled, this opinion may have changed.)

MacArthur ended his message to Arnold with a plea: "In order to meet '0' on more equal terms we consider essential that a more suitable type fighter be allocated this theater [southwest Pacific area]. Since both Jap fighters and bombers can operate above the rated performance altitude of P-40s and P-39s, altitude is an absolute necessity for aircraft in this theater."[14]

Ford Contemplated Mass-Producing P-40s

By mid-1940 the Air Corps noted with concern the need for greater aircraft production rates. Among ideas given consideration was to engage the giant American automobile industry in the business of mass-producing aircraft, since they obviously knew how to mass produce cars. A P-40 was flown to Detroit to permit appropriate staff at Ford Motor Company to inspect the Curtiss machine. Ford officials were confident they could turn out P-40s at the rate of one per hour, if the design could be "frozen" with no further changes. Ultimately, Ford did not get the nod to build P-40s and went into production of B-24s instead.

Tests and Modifications

The Curtiss P-40 series underwent a deliberate evolution on the drawing board and the production line, plus a host of often localized, specialized, adaptations in the field throughout World War II. Inventiveness kept Warhawks in the fray after their primary mission as air-to-air fighters was largely relinquished to other, faster fighters. Changes to production aircraft could mean delays in deliveries as the assembly line stopped at some point to assimilate the change. This dilemma ensued for most production aircraft: Should quantity output be maintained at the expense of improved variants, or should deliveries lag, if need be, to allow improvements to be inserted on the production floor? The P-40 program got caught up in this knotty problem. Combat experience demanded changes if the P-40 was to remain competitive, and field commanders clamored for factory-made improvements. But even as the upgraded P-40s began arriving overseas after a lag in production made necessary by the inserted improvements, the sometimes-serpentine logistics pipeline did not furnish all of the supporting materials for the new models simultaneously, to some extent negating the advantages expected with the revised P-40 aircraft.[15]

The litany of P-40 tests and adaptations recounts modifications that were documented; the very nature of Yankee ingenuity, and the crush of wartime events in remote locations, created the need for many more expedient changes to Warhawks that escaped official notice. Herewith, a telling of some of the projects that altered the way the Warhawk could fight.

Rockets' Red Glare

In June 1942, the U.S. Army's Ordnance Department urged the AAF to capitalize on an experimental 4.5-inch rocket that might be adaptable for air-to-ground use. Launched from a tube, the rocket was first mounted on a P-40 and flown to the Army's Aberdeen Proving Ground in Maryland for ground-firing trials, where blast effects made this installation less than ideal. A different installation was successfully air-fired on 6 July 1942, opening the way for 4.5-inch rocket tests on a variety of fighters and small bombers. It would be more than a year before problems with the rockets themselves were ironed out by the Army; in the meantime, the tube launchers were upgraded from steel to lighter plastic, and meetings were held with various aircraft manufacturers in an effort to standardize the rocket mounts for ease of production.[16]

P-40s of the 74th Fighter Squadron of the 23rd Fighter Group in China made Air Force history when they loosed the first USAAF rockets fired in combat in World War II on 4 March 1944. The rocket-launching Warhawks had the benefit of attention from First Lieutenant John M. Colmant, an aircraft ordnance liaison officer from Wright Field, who accompanied the initial shipment of rockets and tubes to the China-Burma-India Theater (CBI). The rockets, fuses, and a mix of steel and plastic launcher tubes traveled by rail and air to get the ordnance supplies to Kweilin.

The P-40D was the first of the line to use an Allison engine with external spur reduction gearing that allowed a shorter nose with a raised thrust line, defining future P-40 contours. The four wing guns were beefed up to .50-caliber and the nose guns were removed. *Author collection*

The P-40E improved on the similar D-model by increasing the armament to six .50-caliber wing guns, photographed during night test firing with the tail elevated to bring the guns level. With 2,320 E-models built, this was the second most numerous variant of the P-40, eclipsed in numbers only by the P-40N. *Bowers collection*

The target for the baptismal rocket-firing mission was a Japanese-held airfield on Hainan Island. Tube launchers were on hand to equip eight Warhawks with six rockets apiece. Some of the pioneering P-40 rocket-firing pilots experienced difficulties with the circuitry and switching in place that mission; others glowingly described watching the rockets streak into the target area, exploding among buildings and parked aircraft. On the flight home, one of the P-40s was bounced by a Zero and the Warhawk flier elected to jettison his rocket tubes over a bay to better enable him to flee or fight with his P-40. Lieutenant Colmant said after this first rocket-firing P-40 mission, "The general reaction of all the pilots indicated highest approval of the performance of the initial rockets used in combat, and [they] are desirous of obtaining further missions employing their use."[17]

Fourteenth Air Force commander Gen. Claire Chennault told USAAF chief Gen. Hap Arnold that lessons learned during the first mission, when the rocket-spewing P-40s attacked in line-abreast formation, included the need for a more flexible attack formation allowing freedom of movement. Later missions allowed for this, sometimes sending the rocket-laden Warhawks over the target in smaller two-ship line abreast cells, launching rockets and strafing with machine guns in unison. One subsequent rocket strike became a guns-only melee when eight P-40s were jumped early into the mission by Japanese fighters, and all eight Warhawk pilots jettisoned their still-loaded rocket tubes to better meet the air-to-air threat at hand. General Chennault said, "In general the rocket installations to fighters appear satisfactory in all missions."[18]

P-40 on Skis

Before American entry into World War II, the prospect of insinuating ever-more-capable airpower into a cold climate led to the development of snow skis in a fixed streamlined installation on a radial-engine Curtiss P-36, the lineal antecedent of the P-40 series. The fixed installation penalized the speed attainable in the P-36 by 25 to 30 miles per hour, but flight and service testing of the old P-36 was encouraging enough to set in motion construction of retractable skis for a P-40 in January 1942. Where the fixed skis were blunt aerodynamic shapes in an effort at streamlining for flight, retractable skis could be thinner, since their aerodynamic efficiency depended on stowage rather than streamlining in a fixed position.

As first mated to the P-40, the skis when retracted were still far enough from the undersurface of the wing to cause excessive loss of speed, and degraded flying maneuverability, although they were adequate for ground handling. The design of these first skis mandated considerable stand-off from the lower surface of the wing even when retracted; a large aluminum "bathtub" fairing shrouded the ski when retracted, but drag was excessive. At 10,000 feet, these skis penalized the P-40 with a 23-mile-per-hour drop in speed; it was less at other altitude and speed combinations. An AAF tester noted that with the first set of P-40 skis, longitudinal stability was bad, and "the airplane had a tendency to skid one way or another at all speeds at all times." The standard P-40 main landing gear feature of twisting 90 degrees while retracting backward could not be utilized with skis, so the pinion gear that rotated the strut was disconnected, allowing the strut to retract backward into the wing while keeping the toe of the ski pointed forward. The skis stayed horizontal through the retraction cycle. A small tail ski retracted close to the aft fuselage without additional fairing.[19]

The second set of P-40 skis snugged up closer to the aircraft when retracted. This necessitated only a small plywood fairing between the main skis and the wing, greatly improving flight performance. The maximum speed loss was now only 15 miles per hour; longitudinal stability and other flight characteristics were not impaired. A report summarizing the second set of P-40 skis noted, "Tests of the modified P-40 ski installation proved that the airplane handled exceptionally well on the ground in all types of snow encountered, varying from hard-packed snow with icy surface to fresh snow 8 to 12 inches deep. Short radius turns were easily made and the airplane taxied easily through deep snow." USAAF testers pronounced that "retractable skis were feasible and practical from both an aerodynamic and mechanical standpoint." From this start, tests were made with a ski-equipped P-38, P-47, P-51, and a P-63, but this was a feature ultimately not used in combat by the USAAF.[20]

Seeking handling improvements, NACA worked with Curtiss and devised a 20-inch fuselage extension for some P-40Fs and other models. Pitch moment remained the same; fin and rudder moved farther aft. *NACA via Peter M. Bowers collection*

Rolling in a Dive

Warhawk pilots recounted a tendency of P-40s to roll during high-speed dives. This was doubly troubling considering fast dives were a trademark of the rugged Warhawk when setting the stage for its air-to-air combats against admittedly more-maneuverable Japanese fighters. When Curtiss representative Henry Fadden arrived in Australia in March 1943, he quickly tallied AAF Warhawk types in service with the Fifth Air Force at the time: some P-40E-1s originally intended for export, and some P-40Ks with the modified vertical fin. He noted, "Some P-40E-1 aeroplanes still show their unfavorable rolling tendencies in high-speed dives but the pilots do admit better directional and lateral stability in P-40K aeroplanes with the forward-extended vertical stabilizer." In fact, one P-40E in the Fifth Air Force exhibited such drastic rolling characteristics in high-speed dives that the aircraft suffered "serious buckling of the forward edge of the rudder to such an extent that strengthening of the forward vertical beam became necessary." Other P-40s, after logging about 200 hours in the Pacific, showed signs of warped aileron trailing edges as the ailerons were taxed trying to keep the diving Warhawks from rolling. The pilots had already heard about long-fuselage P-40s being built in the States; they anticipated these as the ultimate in correcting the diving dilemma.[21]

Cracking a Window

To facilitate defrosting, P-40s after the early C-model had a thin flat outer front windscreen separated by a small air space from a thick laminated bullet-resistant slab of glass. In field conditions in the Pacific, the thin outer panes cracked, and dust between the two glass panels was a housekeeping chore and a pilot visibility concern. In a few cases, the expedient thing to do was to remove the outer thin glass entirely.[22]

Gun Blast Tubes Were Vital

Metal blast tubes that enclosed the wing-mounted .50-caliber machine guns of P-40s provided a vital function, as some Fifth Air Force armorers learned the hard way. On occasion, rivets wobbled loose in the wing bulkheads near the gun bays. A Curtiss representative noted, "This condition was (stated to have been caused) by firing a sighting shot at a target without installing the gun blast tube. . . . Armament personnel were specifically warned against firing as much as a single round without first installing a gun blast tube." The potent .50-caliber machine gun that eviscerated enemy aircraft could be a danger to the P-40s mounting these weapons due to dramatic pressure rises from muzzle blasts of the mighty .50s.[23]

Pacific P-40 Miscellany

A fact-finding expedition to the South Pacific by Curtiss representative Fadden in March 1943 gleaned insight into Warhawk idiosyncrasies out there: One squadron modified a centerline drop tank to house a reel and line for a tow target, which was snugged to the outside of the drop tank when not deployed. "The bomb-arming control releases a 'chute which pulls out a target and upon completion of the mission the cable and target are released over the runway," Fadden relayed.

P-40 specialists continued to rail against the high-speed wheel landings fighter pilots tended to make in Warhawks; the design was intended for a three-point, tail-low landing to avoid excessive shock on the main landing gear struts. After visiting an Australian P-40 unit in Milne Bay, Fadden reported, "Pilots admitted landing . . . with airspeeds of 110 to 115 miles per hour with the tail in full flying position. I emphatically discouraged this practice as landing gear troubles may certainly be anticipated unless these pilots learn to at least approach a three-point landing."[24]

Nor was P-40 main gear the only one with the potential for problems in the field—tail wheel doors had an annoying habit of drooping in flight, Pacific pilots told the Curtiss representative. Any drop in hydraulic pressure could be enough to allow the doors to droop, and in some instances, the tail wheel approached full extension as well. "It happens so often that a pilot flying in formation often notices his wingman's tail wheel doors open," stated one pilot.[25]

Australians flying K-models said longer shoulder harness straps needed to be installed. "Since pilots are operating over water much of the time," Fadden said, "the Australians have a small dinghy life raft which attaches to the seat-pack type parachute. This raises the pilot too high to use the shoulder straps."[26]

Tanks for More Range

In July 1944 the commanding general of V Fighter Command wanted to know the feasibility of extending the range of P-40Ns by lashing up three drop tanks—one on the centerline and one under each wing. The engineering section of the Fifth Air Force's 49th Fighter Group set to work on the project; range was always a bugaboo, especially in some of the overwater Pacific campaigns. The 49th Group's engineering officer explained a quirk of N-model Warhawks, "On the P-40N airplane, facilities were incorporated in the manufacturer's design to install external wing tanks. This, however, was intended to be used without the ordinary belly tank." Thwarted by the standard of either one or two drop tanks only, the 49th's engineering section routed plumbing and connected the P-40's fuel tanks in a way that permitted the use of drop tanks on all three hard points under the P-40N. To ensure even consumption from both wing drop tanks, thereby preserving optimum flight characteristics, a gasoline tank air vent was modified to guarantee about two pounds of pressure in the external tanks, working along with gravity to keep the fuel pumps drawing evenly from both drop tanks.[27]

The 49th Fighter Group answered the question affirmatively; the field-modified P-40N, under control of pilot First Lieutenant Philip Criechbaum, tucked its landing gear up at 9:10 in the morning, flying nonstop until 4:45 that afternoon—7 hours and 35 minutes in a Warhawk! Lieutenant Criechbaum kept the P-40's airspeed at 170 miles per hour until the external tanks were jettisoned; thereafter he nudged the Warhawk up to 200 miles per hour. The test hop was repeated several times, with the group engineering officer reporting, "From experiments it was found that the P-40 with [three] external fuel tanks has a safe

Close-up photo depicted empennage placement on short fuselage P-40F. *Bowers collection*

Rearward placement of vertical fin and rudder is a telltale sign of long-bodied P-40s, as depicted on a P-40F in 1942. *Bowers collection*

range of 1,300 miles with 60 gallons [of] reserve fuel."[28] At least in tests, the old P-40 could be given long legs.

Warhawk to the 'Nth' Degree

The Army Air Forces Proving Ground at Eglin Field, Florida, wrung out a pair of new P-40N-1s in April 1943 to determine this model's operational suitability. The sample N-models were the first and second of this variant built, serials 42-104429 and 42-104430. Fitted with only four wing guns apiece, the lightened P-40Ns under test carried up to 120 gallons of gasoline internally, and could tank an extra 75 gallons in a centerline drop tank.[29]

While the testers noted that the reduced armament and internal fuel tankage gave the P-40N-1 performance superior to any previous model P-40, they said the new N-models were nonetheless "generally inferior to all other current types of fighters tested at this station." The Eglin evaluators were succinctly blunt in their assessment, "The P-40N-1 is of a design which is believed to have reached its limit in performance unless major changes in control surface design, wing form, structure and horsepower are made." The old war horse had evolved as far as it could. General handling and performance of the stripped-down early P-40Ns were described in the Eglin evaluation: "The P-40N-1 has the best performance of the P-40 series from sea level to approximately 20,000 feet. Here the P-40L with two-stage blowers takes over in performance. Handling characteristics are similar to the P-40E and P-40F. Rate of climb, speed, and turn are improved."[30]

Other items stripped from the P-40N-1 to lighten it included the starter motor, gyro compass, artificial horizon, climb indicator, suction gauge, and carburetor temperature gauge. A smaller battery was furnished. The remaining Spartan accessories contributed to a longer time required to launch a P-40N-1, the evaluators said, due to the need for hand-cranking. The testers also urged a return to six wing guns as necessary for air-to-air and air-to-ground combat.[31]

If the report on P-40N-1 operational suitability found this Warhawk aging, it did record one remarkable feat, "The P-40N-1 has the best turning circle of the current type U.S. fighters. The next best is the P-39N-0, followed by the P-51A." In a dive the P-40N-1 required heavy rudder application "to keep ship in trim," said to make this variant of the Warhawk "not satisfactory [as a gun platform] due to change in rudder trim with speed." The view over the nose, important in deflection shooting where a fighter pilot may actually lose sight of his properly targeted prey, was poorer than in a Merlin-engined P-40F due to the nose carburetor air scoop on the P-40N (and other Allison-engined Warhawks). "Normal acrobatics may be performed," the evaluators reported, "but require excessive strength on controls due to high stick and rudder force." Operational ceiling, at least on the evaluated examples, was

An enlarged dorsal fin characterized the short-fuselage P-40K. Pictured on 9 July 1942 is a P-40K-1 intended for the British, with serial FR241 on the fuselage, but no roundels. In Royal Air Force service, the P-40K was known as the Kittyhawk III.

limited to 25,000 feet because of ignition problems in the V-1710-81 engine.[32]

When describing pilot comfort in the new N-model, the evaluators' summation was to the point, "Similar to the P-40F series. Drafty cockpit." And speed of servicing the P-40N-1, the testers noted perhaps wryly, was "slightly improved over P-40F due to less gas and four guns." With that, they urged reinstatement of the extra pair of guns, and an increase in fuel tankage.[33]

A Pacific Champion of Late-Model P-40s

The men of the 45th Fighter Squadron of the 15th Fighter Group, a 7th Air Force P-40 unit, took it upon themselves to expand the bomb-carrying envelope of their P-40N-5-CUs before any official technical data was available to them. Wanting to see more combat in the central Pacific than they were then getting, the P-40 pilots of the 45th Squadron "desired to attract attention to the versatility of the airplane and thereby be moved to the forward bases," explained 45th Squadron commanding officer Lieutenant Colonel Julian E. Thomas in February 1944. The squadron additionally wanted "to prove to the many unbelievers that the P-40N when compared with any other aircraft in this area was not an outmoded airplane," he added. To do this, the squadron began with bomb load tests devised with several assumptions: "The airplane came equipped with a B-7 bomb shackle under each wing; the maximum given load of a B-7 shackle is approximately 1,100 pounds. Since gas lines could be run out to the wing racks it was assumed that they could each support at least a 75-gallon belly tank. The racks were therefore assumed capable of carrying 500-pound bombs. Since the basic design of the P-40N-5-CU is still approximately the same as older models it was assumed that a gross weight of 11,000 to 12,000 pounds would not seriously impair the flight characteristics of the aircraft."[34]

Following bombing trials with a pair of P-40s carrying three 100-pound bombs on centerline and wing stations, Lieutenant Colonel Thomas, squadron commander, took a P-40 aloft from Apamama with two 500-pound bombs plus a 75-gallon belly tank, flying to Makin and back before dropping the bombs, with enough gasoline left over to make another return trip. Soon, the squadron moved P-40N-5-CUs to Makin, the squadron commander reported, "where they made numerous dive-bombing strikes to Mille atoll and Jaluit atoll with the 2x 500-pound bomb load plus belly tank."[35]

Clearly visible is late style aft glazing on P-40N-40 number 44-47860. This aircraft was the first to be built without camouflage paint—it was painted silver. It was photographed 20 October 1944. *Peter M. Bowers collection*

The eager beavers of the 45th Fighter Squadron next seized upon forthcoming technical information that indicated the P-40 wing racks were stressed to hold a hefty 225-gallon ferry tank. Lieutenant Colonel Thomas tested this out by taking off in a P-40 from Makin with two 1,000-pound SAP bombs plus a belly tank. "Except for feeling heavy," he noted, "the airplane acted normal in level flight and in a dive." Now the squadron put heavyweight P-40s to the acid test of combat, "Two strikes of 16 airplanes each were made to Jaluit with the 2x 1,000-pound SAP bomb load. Although this is a trip of at the very least 700 statute miles, no gas shortage was experienced." The P-40 fliers quickly learned with so much weight suspended from the wings of their Warhawks, "a dive-bombing run had to be on the target from the peel-off since the airplane gained speed so rapidly and was so inherently heavy that major corrections in a dive were next to impossible. In one instance, Lieutenant Morey pulled out of a steep dive with little trouble; the bomb racks bulged a little but have not, as yet, required replacement." Next came skip-bombing runs with both 500-pounders and 1,000-pound bombs on P-40s, at speeds in excess of 400 miles per hour.[36]

The 45th Fighter Squadron report chronicling its heavyweight bombing exploits in the Pacific said, "Belly tanks are always dropped in skip bombing runs in order to get maximum speed." But for other types of sorties, the 45th Squadron had a practice of keeping empty belly tanks attached to the centerline whenever feasible "due to their shortage and due to the danger of the fuel selector sticking and allowing the gas to siphon out the open belly tank pipe." The squadron found the belly tank inconsequential in altering characteristics of dives, saying, "speeds in excess of 450 miles per hour with violent evasive action have been common."[37]

The squadron was enthusiastic in its praise for the P-40N-5, which brought back some features earlier deleted on the P-40N-1. High diving speed and a range of more than 1,000 miles endeared the N-5 model to these Pacific fliers. That remarkable turning ability noted the previous year at Eglin Field was cited again by Lieutenant Colonel Thomas, "The maneuvering qualities compared with a P-39Q-1 are very good; the P-40N with a 75-gallon belly tank can maneuver with an unencumbered P-39Q-1." Candidly, he added, "The P-40N-5-CU is no world beater in straight and level speed (320 miles per hour at sea level, military power, is maximum)." The 45th Fighter Squadron next turned its attentions to operating P-40Ks with 500-pound bombs. "The P-40K is harder to handle and a little more unreliable than the P-40N under this load condition," Lieutenant Colonel Thomas said.[38]

The bubble-topped XP-40Qs benefited from Allison V-1710-121 engines with two-stage superchargers and refinements that made them the fastest Warhawks at 422 miles per hour, but production of Q-models was not to happen. *Bowers collection*

The line-up of Curtiss' wartime contributions shows huge twin-engine C-46 Commando transports looming large over rows of olive P-40Ns and silver-painted N-models. Anticipated postwar civil market for new C-46s did not materialize, and the dated P-40 was not a springboard to future fighter developments for the company. *Bowers collection*

Still not resting, the squadron mounted M-1 bazooka launchers on a P-40N-5-CU, attached to the outboard shackles' sway braces, and wired to fire when the gun camera button was pressed. Bazooka rocket projectiles were successfully fired at various speed and dive angle combinations, up to 70 degrees. But this munition was not as potent as the larger rockets being used in China as of March 1944. The bazooka strapped to P-40 wings "possesses such a low muzzle velocity that its trajectory is tricky and requires a great deal of practice to perfect the firing technique. It is not believed that the damage that would be inflicted from this small rocket would compensate for the trouble and expense of training."[39]

What Price Victory?

Army Air Forces statistics tracked many costs of World War II. The average unit cost for P-40s was lower than for any other Air Force fighter for most of the war years. The sheer volume of P-40 production accounts in part for the low price; a relatively simple design, lacking turbosupercharging, may be another factor. The ability of the P-40 as a ground-attack weapon, coupled with its low price, goes a long way toward explaining why this Curtiss design was kept in production as late as it was, posting a wartime low unit cost of $44,892 in 1944. As chronicled in the *Army Air Forces Statistical Digest—World War II*, available production and cost statistics for fighters included:

Average Unit Cost

	1939–41	*1942*	*1943*	*1944*	*1945*
P-38	$134,284	120,407	105,567	97,147	—
P-39	$ 77,159	69,534	—	50,666	—
P-40	**$ 60,562**	**59,444**	**49,449**	**44,892**	**—**
P-47	$113,246	105,594	104,258	85,578	83,001
P-51	$ —	58,698	58,824	51,572	50,985

Factory Acceptances

	1940	*1941*	*1942*	*1943*	*1944*	*1945*	*TOTAL*
P-38	1	205	1,265	2,213	4,186	1,666	9,536[40]
P-39	13	926	1,973	4,947	1,729	—	9,588
P-40	**778**	**2,246**	**4,454**	**4,258**	**2,002**	**—**	**13,738**
P-47	—	1	526	4,157	6,988	3,559	15,231
P-51	—	138	634	1,710	6,908	5,111	14,501[41]

In November of 1941, the Air Force had 755 P-40s—by far the most numerous fighter type in the inventory.[42]

American aircraft production figures from July 1940 to August 1945 totaled a staggering 295,959 airplanes of all types. Such figures are nearly incomprehensible in an era when total purchases of the B-2 bomber to date are 21 aircraft. In that earlier epoch of vast quantities of warplanes, Curtiss ranked fourth among the top 15 American manufacturers in terms of numbers of aircraft built; only North American Aviation, Consolidated-Vultee (Convair), and Douglas Aircraft produced more units.[43] More than 13,000 P-40s helped put Curtiss that high up on the list.

Warhawks Around the World

Easy to caricature with its deep-chinned radiator inlet, many-paned canopy, and strong wings with noticeable forward sweep along the trailing edges, the P-40 was an icon in its own time, an image of scrappy American fliers and visceral verification that the United States with all its bounty and productivity was, after all, the Arsenal of Democracy. Since before direct American involvement in World War II, P-40s were in service, continuing to the end of the war with American Allies in the Pacific.

When the Royal Air Force took P-40 variants into combat, they helped to forge and validate Air Marshal Arthur Coningham's concept of an effective aerial force, responsive to, but not chained to, ground armies in the sands and stark

Major John Chennault, son of the Flying Tigers' Claire Chennault, adopted a tiger head logo for his Aleutian Tigers, the 11th Fighter Squadron he commanded. *Air Force/Marty Isham collection*

Group portrait by an Aleutian Tiger P-40 shows, not unexpectedly, some irregularity in the application of tiger head to both sides of the aircraft, as evidenced where the designs meet on the top of the cowling. *Air Force*

mountains of North Africa. By 1942, USAAF P-40s contributed firepower to Coningham's combat brew, further cementing his title as a father of air superiority and ground attack doctrine.

Above a bucolic China that must have seemed glacially slow to young American volunteer fighter pilots, Tomahawks and Warhawks under the leadership of the persistent Claire Chennault established a string of victories over a variety of Japanese warplanes, and earned for all time the P-40's instant recognition as a symbol of those brave Flying Tigers. Back in the States, black aviators—the Tuskegee Airmen—waged war on prejudice as they learned to fly P-40s in a previously white USAAF flying fraternity. When the first of the Tuskegee Airmen went overseas to fight the Germans, it was with Curtiss P-40s.

A far-flung net of USAAF historians, many of them performing a task in addition to some other skill, filed ongoing reports on flimsy, carbon-copied paper to create a monumental record and data base on the activities of the Air Force abroad and at home throughout World War II. Capitalizing on the wealth of such information archived at Maxwell Air Force Base, Alabama, compilers Kit Carter and Robert Mueller distilled the substantial *Combat Chronology, 1941–1945; U.S. Army Air Forces in World War II.* This diary of an Air Force at war meticulously recorded the growth and evolution of USAAF fighting power throughout the war, including the spikes of excitement as well as the dutiful day-in, day-out grind of P-40 operations around the world. From Carter and Mueller's groundbreaking volume, as well as a host of other sources, an overview can be derived of the Warhawk at war.

Sometimes the Warhawks flew fighter escort for bombers on raids during which the P-40s also poured fire into the bombers' targets rather than merely flying top cover, thereby compounding the P-40s' contribution to the war effort. Popular names associated with the P-40 series changed. Early models up to the P-40C equivalent were commonly known as Tomahawks. Starting with the model equivalent to the USAAF P-40D, British export variants of this Curtiss fighter were dubbed Kittyhawks. Historian Peter M. Bowers says the name Warhawk was first applied by Curtiss to Merlin-engined variants to differentiate them from their Allison-powered stablemates. Historian Ray Wagner says that in January 1942 all USAAF P-40s were simply called Warhawks. In this narrative, USAAF P-40s of all types (and using either powerplant) referenced after January 1942 will be called Warhawks. And even the globe-girdling Air Force historians and their descendants couldn't tabulate every P-40 operation in a single volume. Sometimes, P-40s flew more than one mission a day, adding to the count. So, with some slight caveats, what follows is a war diary of the Warhawk that offers a representative overview of the service rendered by this durable American fighter:

1941

Even as waves of Japanese warplanes continued to arrive over Oahu the morning of 7 December 1941, USAAF P-40B Tomahawks leapt into the sky to challenge the new foe. Second Lieutenant George Welch of the 47th Pursuit Squadron downed four Japanese aircraft that morning over Hawaii; the attacking fleet lost a total of 20 airplanes.[44] Another stalwart young fighter pilot who mounted a Tomahawk that morning in Hawaii was Lieutenant Francis "Gabby" Gabreski. He did not score any victories on 7 December, but he later scoured the skies over Europe in a massive P-47 Thunderbolt, downing German aircraft and distinguishing himself by achieving multiple-ace status.[45]

News of the surprise raid on Pearl Harbor reached the Philippines, on the other side of the International Dateline, only a half hour before USAAF P-40s were airborne in the early morning darkness in a fruitless attempt to seek out a formation of unknown aircraft painted by radar at Iba Field. A little after noon that first day (8 December for the Philippines), Japanese aircraft attacked Clark Field. Some P-40s scrambled to meet the attackers, and P-40 flier R. L. Keator of the 20th Pursuit Squadron claimed the first Japanese airplane downed over the Philippines. Meanwhile, when the P-40s from Iba returned to that base after not locating the inbound Japanese formation, they found the airfield under attack. Although the enemy bombers were able to drop their loads at Iba, the return of the P-40s meant the Japanese could not afford to strafe the airfield at low level; this lessened the damage at Iba. Even with P-40 opposition, the Japanese managed to dull the ability of the USAAF in the Philippines that first day of war.

Nichols Field in the Philippines was the target of a 9 December Japanese air raid; in the first two days of a brand-new war in the Philippines, about 55 P-40s were destroyed in the air and on the ground. Some remaining P-40s teamed with outmoded Seversky P-35s and with B-17 bombers to attack a Japanese troop convoy intending to put forces ashore at Vigan and Aparri in Luzon on 10 December. The American air fleet was a game, if tattered, remnant of the Far East Air Forces (FEAF). Three days later, First Lieutenant Boyd D. Wagner used a new P-40E to clear four Japanese warplanes from the humid skies near Aparri. Lieutenant Wagner, out to do the job for which he had trained, entered the record books on 14 December 1941 when he shot down his fifth Japanese aircraft, and earned recognition as the AAF's first ace of World War II.

B-17 heavy bomber assets were in painfully short supply during the early fighting in the Philippines. Two days before Christmas 1941, 12 P-40s relinquished dogfighting to team with 6 P-35s in strafing Japanese troops going ashore at San Miguel Bay. Though coolant system battle damage would be a vulnerability with liquid-cooled aircraft like the P-40, its generally robust structure suited it from the start for participation in ground attack sorties.

1942

New P-40s sailed aboard ships bound for the Far East; the beleaguered 17th Pursuit Squadron picked up a baker's dozen of the fighters in Australia and flew them to Java by 25 January 1942 to meet the thrust of the Japanese threat to the region. The AAF P-40s readily engaged in ground

This P-40F hack aircraft used by the 461st Bomb Group at Torretto Air Base, Italy, in 1945 may be a former fighter from the 69th Fighter Squadron of the 57th Fighter Group, possibly serial 41-14596. (See also *Curtiss P-40 in Action* by Ernest R. McDowell, P. 26.) *Photography by Stan Staples*

attack as well as air-to-air operations, slowing a Japanese troop reinforcement at Quinauan Point in early February, escorting ill-fated A-24 Dauntless dive-bombers later in the month, and confronting Japanese bombers over Java.

Even Australia was not immune from the rolling inertia of the Japanese forces; on 19 February 1942, Japanese planes attacked the port city of Darwin, seeking out troop ships in a convoy. Ten P-40s flown to Darwin to provide convoy protection were bagged by the Japanese force.

Events collided in the early days of the war as the Japanese sought to increase and solidify their holdings before an effective Allied response could be fully implemented. On 27 February, the Battle of Java Sea erupted around a Japanese convoy consisting of about 80 ships steaming southwest toward Java, as all available P-40s rose with LB-30s, B-17s, and A-24s in attacks that ultimately had little effect. Still the enemy juggernaut moved forward. Fifth Air Force personnel forced to evacuate Tjilatap had to dispose of 27 crated P-40s delivered there; these brand-new fighters were destroyed to prevent their use by the Japanese. When the importance of a single P-40 loss was magnified by the number and diversity of missions imposed on it early in the war, the sinking of the aged aircraft carrier U.S.S. *Langley,* ferrying 32 P-40s from Australia, was a huge blow.

A meager shadow force of P-40s remained airworthy on Bataan by early March 1942; on the second day of that month, their number dropped by four during some otherwise successful anti shipping sorties in Subic Bay. Even as setbacks dimmed prospects in the Philippines in 1942, the inexorable pulse of new supplies from the United States saw a welcome shipment of 10 P-40s make it to Karachi from Australia by 12 March. And in the Alaska Territory's Aleutian Islands, the 11th Air Force's XI Fighter Command had deployed P-40s and other fighters to Umnak and Cold Bay by late May, with Royal Canadian Air Force (RCAF) Kittyhawk versions flying out of Fort Richardson, Alaska, to challenge developing Japanese moves into this frigid back route into Canada and the United States. The Japanese choreographed two thrusts, one to the Aleutians and one to Midway, in this time period.

War came to Alaska on 3 June when red-insignia-emblazoned Japanese planes targeted

Variations in paint and markings adorn two Merlin Warhawk hacks kept by the Liberator-equipped 484th Bomb Group in Italy.
Photography by Stan Staples

Dutch Harbor and Fort Mears. Eleventh Air Force P-40s rose to the occasion, but most did not connect with the enemy that day. The Curtisses sent from Cold Bay reached the scene of battle 10 minutes after the last wave of Japanese departed; a communications failure denied the Umnak-based P-40s the timely alert needed to be effective. But soon a reconnaissance force of nine P-40s and six B-26 Marauders, looking in vain for the Japanese surface fleet, bore some fruit as two P-40s engaged four Japanese carrier-based aircraft, claiming a kill on one enemy plane and scoring damage on another in the cold skies.

Japanese bombers in several waves attacked lonely Dutch Harbor the next day. Two P-40s challenged four bombers before noon over Umnak Pass, sending three of the Japanese warplanes plunging earthward for the last time. The first combat casualty for the 11th Air Force was posted that afternoon following a melee between Warhawks and nine enemy fighters, which resulted in a one-for-one trade of downed aircraft.[46]

For a time in the uncertain summer of 1942, USAAF Warhawks in Alaska assumed an importance that belies their small numbers in that theater. In June and July, the American P-40 tally in the Alaska Territory was 51 and 50 aircraft, respectively. By August the following year, the highwater mark of USAAF P-40s in Alaska was posted at 124 Warhawks.[47]

If Alaska was a feint in force by the Japanese to divert attention away from their real goal of scoring a decisive victory at Midway, the effort was wasted. A combined AAF, Navy, and Marine Corps defense of Midway, crowned by uncannily successful attacks on Japanese aircraft carriers by Navy SBDs, set in motion the Allied engine of victory that would achieve its purpose by late summer 1945. But the victory at Midway, which would prove so pivotal to the ultimate course of the war, could not be taken as a cause for relaxation at the time. In the summer of 1942, P-40s from the 73rd Fighter Squadron shipped to Midway aboard the carrier U.S.S. *Saratoga,* making a one-way launch from the aircraft carrier before recovering on the island to replace Navy warplanes recently consumed in battle there. The AAF Warhawks quickly set up a pattern of dawn and dusk patrols, scanning the sea and sky for any signs of a return by the Japanese to those waters. This chore, important at first, and later a cause of monotony, would consume the attention of the Midway Warhawks for more than a year until the P-40s were relieved on 23 June 1943.

In China throughout 1942 and well into the first half of 1943, P-40s were considered the only first-line AAF fighters in theater. By December 1942, the number of USAAF P-40s in the China-Burma-India Theater had grown to 180 fighters. These were employed by units including those of the China Air Task Force (CATF), formally activated, intentionally, no doubt, on the Fourth of July 1942. Nonetheless, the impatient demands of combat caused the new CATF to use P-40s as escort to four B-25s on 1 July, inaugurating CATF operations in essence with a bombing raid of little impact on docks at Hankow. The CATF, led by American Volunteer Group hero Chennault, took up the cudgel for his battle-worn Flying Tigers. While some former Flying Tiger P-40s were pressed into CATF service in 1942, not many of their colorful pilots stayed around to man them; only a few AVG pilots and ground personnel chose to join the USAAF when the AVG was disbanded.

On the first official date of CATF operations, 4 July, P-40s checked Japanese fighter-bombers over Kweilin, turning the attackers away and claiming 13 Japanese planes shot down. CATF soon set up missions with P-40s escorting B-25s, and then strafing targets as available. During this time, in the CBI, P-40s were the only dogfighters available to the USAAF, and their record of enemy engagements grew. The story of air operations in the CBI was punctuated by one combatant raiding an important airfield of the other over time in an effort to stop particularly aggravating air attacks. Japanese vulnerability to attacks along the Yangtze River Valley led to a 36-hour bombing campaign against CATF assets at Hengyang starting 30 July 1942. Determined interception by P-40s thwarted most damage to Hengyang's airfield, at a ratio of 3 P-40s to 17 Japanese warplanes lost. In the following month, a trio of CATF P-40s escorted B-25s to Haiphong, where the Warhawks swooped to make attacks as well in CATF's first Indochina raid.

The middle of 1942 saw AAF Warhawks employed in combined air and ground operations against the Japanese in several theaters, as in New Guinea in July, where Warhawks joined P-39s to work over Japanese landing barges and other shipping used by the enemy to promote a Japanese invasion over the intimidating Owen Stanley Mountains. And, by the end of that month, the Warhawk-equipped air echelon of the 57th Fighter Group reported to Palestine, bolstering American presence in the Middle East.[48] In sheer numbers, the fleet of USAAF P-40s in the Mediterranean Theater of Operations (MTO) was a significant player, with a high of 733 American-manned Warhawks listed there by May 1943.[49] By the end of August 1942, the 57th was flying escort. Soon it would be bloodied by encounters with Axis fighters over the desert.

Around the world in 1942, commanders realized the potential of the durable Warhawk for ground attack missions. Its six wing-mounted .50-caliber guns put out a withering, predictable stream of fire set to converge at a predetermined point well in front of the P-40. The other available fighter for ground attack work at this time was the Bell P-39 Airacobra, potent with a 37-millimeter cannon in the nose, but otherwise confounded with a hash of .30-caliber wing guns and .50-caliber cowling guns, each with their own distinct trajectories. While P-39 pilots learned to finesse the strong points of their Airacobras, other fliers preferred the simplicity of the Warhawk's all-.50-caliber armament.

Rugged as it was, the P-40 was not infallible to groundfire, as a hapless student pilot learned in 1945 near Thomasville, Georgia, when a .50-caliber bullet from one of the P-40's guns careened skyward during a strafing run and punctured the coolant radiator of the same aircraft that had fired the round, bringing the Warhawk down in a cornfield. And in the CBI in 1944, an official synopsis of morale in the 23rd Fighter Group contained a telling vignette about the P-40's relative combat merits that late in the war: "During the latter part of 1944 the P-40s remaining in the 23rd Group were replaced with P-51s. This had a stimulating effect upon the pilots inasmuch as they felt that they were better equipped so far as aerial combat was concerned and in fact, with their new aircraft, they were anxious to meet enemy opposition in the air. At the same time they were perhaps a little more apprehensive about being shot down while making strafing attacks since they felt that the new airplanes were more vulnerable to ground fire."[50]

The cadence of combat for the P-40 in the fall of 1942 settled into repeat visits to Japanese shipping points in the South Pacific, sweeps over the land battles of North Africa, and escort/ground attack sorties in the CBI. With other air combat fighters still largely a stateside promise, P-40s also continued to be pressed into dogfights by aggressive young American fliers.

In Alaska, fog-shrouded island targets and rapidly changing meteorological conditions proved to be an enemy mightier than the Japanese, scrubbing entire 11th Air Force operations, like a proposed bombing mission to Kiska on 21 September 1942 that included 20 P-40s in its makeup. The fleet of Warhawks, P-39s, nine B-24s, one LB-30, and a pair of B-17s was thwarted by the weather that day. On the 25th of the month, Royal Canadian Air Force Kittyhawks participated in the 11th Air Force's first combined American-Canadian mission of the war in the Aleutians.[51]

Although not as numerous as their German counterparts, Japanese tanks nonetheless provided targets for marauding Fifth Air Force P-40s, Airacobras, and B-17s roaming the Buna-Kokoda trail in September 1942, as Australian ground forces mustered an offensive to shove the Japanese back along the Port Moresby-Kokoda trail. The year continued with Warhawks shouldering many ground attacks, while still downing Stukas over North Africa and Japanese fighters over Hanoi. By 5 November, German General Erwin Rommel's crack forces were in retreat to the west of El Alamein, harassed by bombing P-40s. Five days later, the aircraft carrier U.S.S. *Chenango,* off the North African coast, launched its cargo of 72 P-40s belonging to the 33rd Fighter Group, eager to join the fray as part of Operation Torch. Increasing numbers of P-40s in North Africa, and an ever-more dismal state of affairs for the Germans there, contributed to an umbrella of Warhawks over the front, supporting the Allies. The size of P-40 formations put aloft continued to grow as the year waned, evidence of American production capacity. Twin-engine P-38 Lightnings began taking some of the fighter missions in North Africa by December 1942, starting an inexorable evolution in USAAF capabilities that would see Warhawks increasingly

New Zealand mechanics used a manual hoist to change the Allison on a Kittyhawk of the RNZAF at Espiritu Santo in July 1943. *Air Force*

used for ground attack missions while other fighters took on enemy aircraft.[52]

1943

Through most of 1943, monthly acceptance rates for new P-40s at the factory were between 300 and 400 aircraft. In January 1943, the AAF had on hand 2,017 P-40s, as evidenced by the increasing magnitude and scope of Warhawk combat operations. To be sure, many P-40s remained in the United States as trainers; 1,365 of the type were listed by the AAF as being overseas assets that month.[53]

Australian and American troops secured Buna Mission on 2 January 1943; the following day, the Fifth Air Force sent P-40s to strafe Japanese troops in nearby waters. If the Japanese were stretched thin along tenuous supply lines in parts of the Pacific, the problem was not unique to them. By the 10th day of January 1943, the CATF had to stand its P-40s down for the rest of the month because of an acute gasoline shortage.

Navigating trackless vistas of the Pacific Ocean was daunting for many new fighter pilots. Often, a B-17 or some other aircraft equipped with a full navigator's station would shepherd fighters to a forward base, as on 23 January when the AAF's longest overwater mass flight to date took place, when two dozen P-40s of the 78th Fighter Squadron flew about 1,100 nautical miles from Barking Sands, Hawaii Territory, to Midway Island. The arriving Warhawks relieved their fellows from the 73rd Fighter Squadron, who had come to Midway the previous summer via aircraft carrier. Within days, the homeward-bound P-40s of the 73rd Squadron bested the overwater record by spanning from Midway to Kaneohe Naval Air Station, a distance of about 1,400 miles.[54]

Some Warhawk missions practiced the art of war with finesse, as on 5 February when 10th Air Force P-40s successfully bombed a railway cut west of Meza and then roared back to machine-gun a train that had been stalled by the demolished tracks. By 21 March, Ninth Air Force units in the Mediterranean were able to post nearly 100 Warhawk sorties, as the number of

RNZAF P-40N nears touchdown at Bougainville in 1944. *Air Force*

fighters reaching the fronts grew. The Mareth battle area in North Africa drew repeat attention from Warhawks throughout this period until the collapse of the Mareth Line by 29 March.

Targets in the CBI could be exotic and archaic; on 5 April 1943, 14th Air Force P-40s flying armed reconnaissance strafed 15 horse-drawn wagons at Wanling; nine days later, 14th AF Warhawks targeted pack horses. Also that month, 10th AF Warhawk fliers were expanding the P-40's utility as a fighter-bomber by carrying a large 1,000-pound bomb beneath each of the Curtiss fighters.

The Mediterranean Sea in the first half of 1943 was shadowed by aircraft of both combatant sides. Several times, USAAF P-40s in the MTO flew sea searches, looking for Axis targets. At other times they flew convoy escort, protecting Allied shipping. The cold realities of warfare demanded that German supply lines to North Africa be interdicted as often and as decisively as possible. On 18 April, Warhawks piloted by men of the Ninth Air Force's 57th Fighter Group intercepted a German movement of transport aircraft near Cape Bon. The P-40s rampaged among the enemy transport and fighter planes, pouring .50-caliber fire into shuddering Luftwaffe airplanes shedding bits of metal and fabric. The 57th Group claimed more than 70 enemy aircraft destroyed in a melee over the Gulf of Tunis that went down in history as the Palm Sunday Massacre. A Distinguished Unit Citation (DUC) subsequently acknowledged the 57th's feat that day.

If latter-day tacticians can contemplate modern air wars in terms of only weeks or even days, their World War II counterparts had no such luxury. The long-haul nature of the Second World War is manifest in a target hit by 14th Air Force P-40s and B-25s on 24 April 1943: Mines and a smelter at Namtu in the CBI were strafed by P-40s; the B-25s dropped bombs. Remote mineral resources, perhaps months away from being of use to the Japanese, were considered vital targets in a Pacific war that lasted the better part of four years.

May 1943 saw MTO P-40s repeatedly engaged in strafing enemy shipping in the Gulf of Tunis and environs; on the ninth day of the month, the swelling resources of Ninth Air Force allowed a tally of more than 300 sorties by Warhawks to be posted. Mixed formations of U.S. and foreign P-40s were not only a feature of Alaska fighting; on 13 May, six Royal New Zealand Air Force (RNZAF) Curtisses joined similar P-40s from the 13th Air Force to intercept about 20 Japanese airplanes in the Tulagi-Russell Islands vicinity. Two days later, up in Kunming, China, a force estimated at 25–35 Japanese bombers escorted by 30–40 fighters was challenged by 28 Warhawks from the 14th Air Force. The P-40 could still give a good account of itself in mid-1943, and claims were made for 13 Japanese fighters and a pair of bombers downed in that confrontation.[55]

In the dank Aleutians, P-40s continued to rise, weather permitting, to strike Japanese forces lodged in Kiska in the first half of 1943. And near the end of May, patrolling Seventh Air Force P-40s from the Hawaiian island of Kauai bombed a submarine from an altitude of 1,500 feet; debris and an oil slick were later noted in the vicinity. The war in the Mediterranean was being deliberately pushed north across the sea toward Sardinia, Panteleria, and other nearby targets as the impending July invasion of Sicily loomed larger by the day.

The last day of May 1943 included a mission by 14th Air Force B-24 Liberators to Ichang, escorted by both USAAF and Nationalist Chinese P-40s. When bounced by about 20 Japanese fighters, the mixed fleet of Warhawks engaged. In the ensuing gun battle, the Liberators and Warhawks claimed five Japanese fighters shot out of the sky; one Chinese P-40 was lost.

The tropic air reverberated to the sound of Allisons as P-40s from USAAF and RNZAF units joined with P-38s and Navy and Marine fighters in intercepting a significant fleet of Japanese dive-bombers and fighter escorts on 7 June in a running battle that extended all the way to Guadalcanal, the intended target of the Japanese force. The mixed formation of Allied warplanes gave up 9 of their number for the downing of more than 20 Japanese planes.

On 12 June, in a remarkable show of airpower, Ninth Air Force P-40s escorted B-25s attacking Lampedusa Island. The island's Axis forces surrendered unconditionally, permitting British Coldstream Guards to come ashore. By 26 June, NAAF's 33rd Fighter Group, a Warhawk outfit, became the first unit to set up operations on Pantelleria as the Allies covered more of the Mediterranean map.

As July opened, with less than two weeks until the planned Allied invasion of Sicily, Ninth Air Force P-40s flew armed reconnaissance along the southern Sicilian coastline; combats with Me-109s ensued, as on the Fourth of July 1943, when four Warhawks fell in combat that also claimed three Me-109s. Warhawks continued to dive-bomb and strafe targets on Sicily, and to escort bombers, in an orchestrated, and largely successful, bid to neutralize Axis airpower in the face of the impending invasion of Sicily. With the invasion in full swing on 10 July, P-40s flew cover for amphibious troop landings, and Warhawks continued to unfurl a protective umbrella over the beaches the following day.[56]

The dispatch of P-40s to bomb Japanese assets in the Aleutians continued in the summer of 1943, as on 24 July when the 11th Air Force logged 62 P-40 sorties in nine missions, including some with RCAF pilots, out to bomb and strafe the runway and anti-aircraft gun emplacements around Kiska. The Warhawks flew into heavy Japanese antiaircraft fire, which brought down a Curtiss fighter that day. They repeated with another call on Kiska the following day, and then on the 26th of the month lost another P-40 to antiaircraft fire.

In the Pacific, Warhawks finished the month of July in a variety of ground attacks. On 30 July, 14th Air Force had 15 P-40s attack 39 Japanese fighters and 24 bombers over Hengyang in a fracas that saw the Warhawk pilots down 5 Japanese warplanes—2 fighters and 3 bombers—for the loss of 2 P-40s; Warhawks were still in the air-to-air campaign.

The pipeline of aircraft from the United States allowed the Ninth Air Force to break its own records repeatedly in this period, as on 3 August 1943 when that organization logged more than 300 Warhawk sorties in attacks on shipping and harbors at Milazzo and Messina, and in support of British troops in the vicinity of Catania-Bronte.

Two days later, NAAF Warhawks escorting B-25s were released from that duty after the B-25s completed their bombing, thereby permitting the P-40s to swoop down low over the sea southwest of Sardinia where they attacked, and possibly sank, a U-boat. The MTO Warhawks often interdicted shipping between mainland Italy and Sicily during this period.[57]

Progress in the Pacific war's prosecution by the Allies was noted on 13 August when a group of four 13th Air Force P-40s were the first Allied aircraft to land on the repaired airfield at Munda, so long a target for Allied bombing until its reclamation from Japanese hands. In the 14th Air Force sphere of influence, dogfights between P-40s and Japanese warplanes were still possible events, as on 20 August when 15 Warhawks challenged a numerically superior force of 21 Japanese fighters over Kweilin. That air battle ended in a destructive draw, with 2 P-40s and 2 Japanese Zeros shot down. The following day, 19 P-40s from the 14th AF clashed with 33 Japanese aircraft, claiming 5 more Zeros shot down. And also on 21 August 1943, the Aleutian campaign closed as the Japanese threat to the North American continent through its frigid back door went away. The Aleutian campaign, starting on 3 June 1942, had cost the 11th Air Force 29 aircraft of all kinds, in exchange for the destruction of 69 Japanese aircraft, 21 enemy ships, and the inflicting of damage on 29 ships.[58]

As many of their brethren continued to target trains, barges, and other forms of enemy transport, on 30 August a mixed bag of the 13th Air Force warplanes that included some P-40s pressed through a screen of Japanese fighters to pummel the airfield at Kahili. Next day, the unflagging Warhawks of 13th Air Force swung into action against Japanese aircraft in a chasing air battle over Vella Lavella, with claims for five downed Japanese planes posted.

NAAF P-40s, transferred to the 12th Air Force on 1 September 1943, bombed a zinc plant at Iglesias and strafed a factory in the vicinity of Gonnesa that day; it was a resource and manufacturing-capacity war even in the MTO. The numbers of USAAF warplanes available by September 1943 had to be a daunting signal to Japanese and German commanders—on 27 September, the Fifth Air Force posted a mixture of 129 Warhawks and P-38s detailed to escort 117 B-24s and B-25s bent on striking shipping and airfields around Wewak. Four days later, in the 10th Air Force's geographic domain, the arrival of the 80th Fighter Group meant several more squadrons of P-40s were on hand. Armed with ever-more complete intelligence information about Japanese fighters, confident 14th Air Force Warhawk pilots on 6 October used a mere 7 P-40s to challenge, and thwart, a Japanese force numbering 27 bombers and 21 fighters. The Warhawks claimed 1 fighter and 1 bomber downed, and the Japanese retreated toward Canton without dropping their bombs.[59]

Warhawks were responsible for opening volleys at Myitkyina on 13 October 1943 in a campaign by the 10th Air Force to neutralize Japanese airstrips in Burma that posed a threat to Hump transport operations. In the South Pacific, the 13th Air Force directed a mission against Kahili airfield on 24 October that melded 24 RNZAF P-40s with 36 B-25s and 4 Corsairs.

By this time, the Warhawk's fight was increasingly in the Pacific and CBI. P-40s would depart remaining 12th Air Force MTO units by mid-1944, but they still made occasional headlines and footnotes over Italy up to that time.[60] (Air-to-air combat involving P-40s was more likely to take place against Japanese forces by this time, although 12th Air Force Warhawks did account for one enemy aircraft downed over the Adriatic Sea on Christmas Eve 1943.) On 28 and 29 November, the 14th Air Force sent Warhawks laden with droppable ammunition and food to bolster Chinese troops under siege at Changte. Despite supply drops and bombing of Japanese targets there by 14th AF P-40s, Changte fell to the Japanese in early December.

1944

Choking snows brought many Axis vehicles to a halt in early January 1944, making it easier for 12th Air Force P-40s to join Spitfires in foraging among idle vehicles in Italy. A German tank repair facility came under Warhawk attack by 12th AF pilots on 14 January, as if to highlight the emphasis of the Italian air campaign against all kinds of ground vehicles. The 16th day of January 1944 saw a remarkable fleet of aging USAAF warplane types—P-40s, P-39s, and A-24 Dauntlesses—all from the Seventh Air Force at Makin, launch an attack on Japanese assets at Mille.

To help teach ground handling of the P-40, this nonflying mascot was fitted with antinoseover gear and used for taxi training. Early P-40 pilots soon found the long-nosed P-40 was easier to tip up on its nose than had been the stubby P-36. *SDAM*

In the MTO, 12th Air Force Warhawks spread the melodious tones of their Allison engines over German targets including trains, wharves, and shipping around Ploca and Metkovic. Nor was the P-40 limited to interdiction in the 12th AF; on 20 January, a mixture of P-40s and A-36s totaled nearly 200 sorties to support the U.S. Fifth Army's 36th Division in an offensive across the Rapido River as other 12th AF Warhawks pinpointed ground targets along the British Eighth Army front.

The 23rd day of January 1944 would prove exciting and demanding for 49th Fighter Group Warhawk pilot Robert DeHaven, who was piloting a P-40N as part of the escort cover for nearly three dozen Liberator bombers bound for Wewak. In the morning light off Moem Point, DeHaven and his cohorts caught sight of 30 to 50 Japanese fighters. Warhawk drop tanks tumbled from the fighters as the AAF pilots made ready to dive on the enemy. DeHaven's flight of P-40s nosed after a Nakajima Ki-43 Hayabusa (Peregrine Falcon) that had made a pass at the Liberators. As the light and maneuverable Hayabusa (code-named Oscar by the Allies) rolled away from DeHaven, he pursued, firing at the Japanese fighter until he had to break off the engagement to avoid ramming the enemy aircraft.[61]

DeHaven converted the speed of his first diving attack into a climb that put him back at altitude with the Liberators he was protecting. From this perch he nosed his P-40N into another dive down to around 10,000 feet to chase off a second Oscar that was challenging another P-40. Scanning through the glazing of his Warhawk, DeHaven caught sight of a pair of Japanese fighters dogging a P-40 low over the water that spread beneath the running combatants. As DeHaven split-S'd his Warhawk to enter that contest, the set-upon Warhawk below him burned and crashed into the sea. Without time to ponder events, DeHaven nosed his N-model Warhawk toward the Hayabusa that had downed the other P-40. As he loosed a torrent of .50-caliber bullets into the Hayabusa, DeHaven did not realize he had engaged Japanese army ace Captain Shigeo

This long-bodied P-40K (hence, no extended dorsal fin) was converted for use as a ground trainer at Sarasota, Florida, when photographed in August 1944. *Air Force via SDAM*

Nango. The Nakajima torched flames along the left side of the fuselage, and Nango was doomed.[62]

It was a clash of equals—if the P-40N had a speed advantage of perhaps 40 miles per hour over the Hayabusa (which topped out at about 330 miles per hour), maneuverability was all on the side of the nimble Nakajima. DeHaven and Nango knew the relative strengths and weaknesses of each other's aircraft. The P-40 could successfully wage a diving attack, breaking off at will; DeHaven would have been at risk had he allowed the fight to become a turning contest, where the Hayabusa's so-called "butterfly flaps" gave it a decided maneuvering edge. Even as both the P-40 and the Ki-43 were aging warriors in 1944, they still were lethal in the hands of brave young pilots.[63]

The new year found 12th Air Force Warhawks alternating between close support of Fifth Army units in the Anzio battlefield region and farther-flung attacks against a variety of enemy transportation. When the Germans launched a powerful counter-offensive at Anzio in early February, some 12th Air Force P-40s were among the few AAF aircraft able to get airborne in inclement weather to render assistance to Fifth Army units. On 7 February, a German railway-mounted gun was targeted by Warhawks from the 12th AF; two days later, the P-40s and A-36s of the 12th Air Force were going after German concentration points vital to the Axis counterattack at Anzio. Except for the pockets of A-36s in Italy and a few A-24s belonging to the Seventh Air Force, fighters like the P-40 had established their primacy as bomb-dropping ground attack weapons.[64]

Increasingly into 1944, the 10th Air Force, and later the 14th Air Force, dispatched mixed groupings of P-40s and P-51 Mustangs, heralding the incoming tide of Mustangs in all theaters. The abundance of Warhawks still meant worldwide use, as on 11 February 1944 when no fewer than five of the USAAF's numbered regional air forces put P-40s aloft in combat. On 15 February, 10th Air Force Warhawks played an unusual role in the fighting when they sowed land mines over Nampaung. The following day, 12th AF P-40s brought to bear an attack on the abbey at Monte Cassino, a sometimes-controversial target in the Italian campaign. By 18 February, the determined German thrust into the Allied Anzio beachhead was at its maximum penetration, as P-40s contributed to blunting the Axis attack. Next day, 12th AF Warhawks and A-36s flew a total of more than 200 sorties in about 20 missions to keep German armor, troops, and transportation preoccupied as an Allied attack again turned the Anzio battle toward an ultimate Allied victory. By 20 February, the Axis ambitions were clearly defeated there; in addition to ground attack sorties, Warhawks sometimes flew protective cover over the battlefield.[65]

During this time, the 14th Air Force sometimes posted mixed Chinese and AAF P-40 missions. The mission compilations show Warhawks all over the world returning to the same targets day in, day out: Mille, Anzio, Myitkyina, Rabaul, Rome, Wewak, and a host of repeated names. World War II was a contest of massive firepower, not precision-guided weapons, making return engagements the norm.

The Warhawk's air combat role was not over in Europe—on 22 March 1944, 12th AF P-40s patrolling Cassino and Anzio claimed two enemy fighters shot down. Even as the Warhawk proved it could still take on enemy planes in the skies over Italy, a buildup of P-47s in that region heralded the decline of P-40 operations in the Mediterranean. As early as 19 March, the 12th Air Force began sorties in support of Operation Strangle, intended to stop German supply trains as far from the fighting as possible. The power of the recently defeated German counterattack at Anzio contributed to the sense of urgency surrounding

This P-40 systems training device shows the bomb release mechanism mounted to a plywood scale sillhouette of Warhawk, 1943. *Air Force*

Operation Strangle, as fighter-bombers, including P-40s, strove to stop German trains far enough from the front lines to keep the supplies from handily reaching the front, while still making the attacks close enough to the front to limit the Germans' choices for alternate routes. Operation Strangle was intended to cripple Italy's famous rail network and force the Germans to rely on highway transport—not a German strong suit there. As Operation Strangle proceeded, a slowdown in ground fighting meant the Germans consumed less war materiel. Though Operation Strangle did not compel the Germans to abandon their Gustav line as had been hoped, it did prove a textbook validation of two-pronged concentrated attacks on rail and road transport.[66]

On 27 April 1944, rocket-firing P-40s from the 14th Air Force paid a call on about 20 junks to the south of Sashi. During the next month, 14th AF target lists for Warhawks included an 18 May strike by 30 P-40s against Japanese troops and positions at Tatangtzu, Tengchung, Mamien Pass, and Luchiangpa, in support of friendly ground forces. In the Far East, Warhawks sometimes found archaic and unusual targets valuable to hit, as when steam rollers were demolished and horses used for transport were strafed.

In an unintended precursor to combat operations of a quarter century later, 16 P-40s and 11 Mitchell bombers from the 14th Air Force roamed over a variety of targets in south China and in Indochina on 12 May 1944; in the 1960s, American airmen would not have such free rein in the region, being bound by restrictive rules of engagement that prohibited entering Chinese airspace. But in 1944, no dotted line between Japanese-occupied Indochina and Japanese-occupied China hindered Warhawk pilots on opportune missions. As early summer temperatures rose in the CBI Theater, P-40s of the 10th and 14th Air Forces occasionally targeted Japanese troops as part of close air support missions to help friendly forces at Mogaung Valley and the Salween area, respectively. The daily lists of Warhawk sorties were exhaustive testimonials to the volume of P-40s in service, and their general durability under fire. Thirteenth and Fifth Air Force P-40s attacked Rabaul and Wewak; the 13th Air Force marked the end of May by sending 12 Warhawks along with 22 Airacobras to savage the enemy supply dumps located near Ratawul.[67]

In June 1944, 14th Air Force P-40s occasionally used air-to-ground rockets in their attacks. The pattern of sustained pressure against enemy strongholds continued, with 10th Air Force P-40s and other combat aircraft repeatedly targeting Myitkyina and Mogaung sites into June and July, even as 14th AF Warhawks returned over the smoking Salween battle front. The 25th of July 1944 found CBI Warhawks tangling with Japanese fighters over Yoyang, as the Japanese tried to intercept a formation of B-24 Liberators. The 27 escorting Warhawks claimed 6 enemy fighters brought to earth.

The taking of Myitkyina, Burma, from the Japanese by General "Vinegar Joe" Stilwell's army by 3 August 1944 followed the capture of its airfield in May. This all was made possible, in part at least, by dogged P-40s attacks against Japanese ground targets there. Fighter-bombers "did the work of howitzers" there because dense jungle foliage limited artillery fields of fire and hindered the registration of the large groundfire rounds, Air Force historians would later note.[68] Perhaps more to the point, there simply weren't sufficient numbers of big Allied guns in the Myitkyina battle mix; fighter-bombers had to supplant artillery. To enhance communication between ground forces and 10th Air Force fighter-bomber pilots, the aviators and troops on the ground were each furnished the same set of photos of the target area with a grid superimposed on clear plastic. This enabled coordination of targets by grid. Once the Myitkyina airfield was secure, a grouping of 8, and then 12, Warhawks moved in even as Japanese troops remained within 1,000 yards of the place. Under fire during takeoffs and landings, the P-40s at Myitkyina dive-bombed the closest machine gun pits, but more distant guns remained a threat. The garrison of Warhawks at Myitkyina undertook many sorties to help liberate the town, sometimes hitting Japanese targets within 75 yards of friendly forces. Other fighter-bombers flew over Myitkyina from bases farther afield, adding their weight to the capture of that town.[69]

A frequent pastime of 14th Air Force P-40 pilots during 1944 was river traffic interdiction. From .50-caliber machine guns in the wings of Warhawks, spinning bullets, a half-inch in diameter, tore into wooden-hulled sampans and junks, splintering even stout watercraft and settling them in their wakes.

Far East Air Forces—FEAF—continued to employ P-40s in ground attack sorties into October 1944; by November, FEAF Warhawks and Liberators were targeting airfields and barges in the central Philippines, as their 14th Air Force counterparts repeatedly swept over south China looking for ground targets. The year drew to a close with this pattern intact; Far East, 10th, and 14th Air Forces each continuing to employ Warhawks in the sometimes arduous, but increasingly promising, prosecution of a far-flung war against Japan.

1945

FEAF Warhawks struck at airfields in the Lingayen Gulf area on 8 January 1945; two days later, FEAF statistics included about 60 P-40 sorties involved in strafing and bombing in the vicinity of Galela. Hong Kong shipping and train targets came under punishment from 14th AF Warhawks on 18 January. Into January, 14th Air Force Warhawks sometimes roamed over the north China plain; locomotives and other forms of Japanese transport continued to suffer as a result. The Japanese were losing their tenacious three-year grip on the Philippines; on 21 February 1945, FEAF Warhawks hit several targets in that region, including storied Corregidor.[70]

The P-40 pilots of the 11th Air Force brought their Warhawks into action on 13 April 1945 when they and their compatriot P-38 fliers were scrambled to intercept unknown radar targets that turned out to be paper Japanese balloon bombs, nine of which were shot down over the western Aleutians by the mixed fleet of responding fighters. In May of 1945, as Japanese forces withdrew from south China, 14th Air Force fighter-bombers including P-40s hunted among the withdrawing enemy forces, crippling their mobility. The aging Warhawk served well into the last year of World War II, its ground-attack abilities not disputed. Clearly, the availability of newer fighter-bombers from the vast industrial capacity of the United States spelled an end to the out-of-production P-40s lingering in AAF service. But the P-40 went out on a positive note, still able to carry the war to the Japanese.

The numbers were telling: By August 1945, only 116 P-40s were still listed on hand in the USAAF, down from their zenith of 2,499 in the AAF in April 1944.[71]

Tigers in the Sky

They were former American military pilots, released from U.S. service at their own request to fight against the Japanese on behalf of Chiang Kai-shek's Chinese forces. They were glorified in newspapers and newsreels, and raised to near mythical status by an archetypal John Wayne movie. Rowdy Marine flier Gregory "Pappy" Boyington had been one of their number, adding his own brand of grit to their reputation. And they were led by square-jawed Claire Chennault, a no-nonsense pilot whose very profile called to mind heroic art of steel-nerved American fliers coolly operating against incredible odds. They were the Flying Tigers—the American Volunteer Group—the AVG. If King Arthur had his knights of the round table, America—and China—had the Flying Tigers.

Late in the summer of 1941, with the United States officially maintaining neutrality, retired USAAF Captain Claire Chennault organized his American Volunteer Group to fight the Japanese in the skies over China. The formation of the American Volunteer Group coincided somewhat with Army Brigadier General John Magruder's U.S. Military Mission to China, formed in the fall of 1941 "to assist China in her struggle against Japan by providing her with American war munitions."[72]

Chennault, who was retired from U.S. military service officially because of a hearing problem, found the Chinese government willing to employ his services as an advisor beginning in 1937. Chennault had been a voice for the aggressive development of pursuit aviation in the U.S. Army

Trusty Tomahawk of the storied Flying Tigers taxies on turf. A pair of machine guns is visible in the left wing. *SDAM*

Air Corps in the 1930s, at a time when strategic bombardment advocates were in ascendancy. Worthy as strategic bombardment was, among many vocal and influential Air Corps planners in that era there existed a dually defeating belief that a formation of bombers could not be intercepted and thwarted. This gave bombardment aviation proponents a false sense of security and made arguments for pursuit aviation seem less worthy. In this atmosphere, the Air Corps began courting the notion of bomber destroyers; large, (and hence relatively slow and ponderous) multiplace gunship aircraft intended to wreak havoc among bomber formations, or alternately protect friendly bombers.

As an instructor in the Air Corps Tactical School, Chennault honed concepts for air defense that depended on an air warning network to alert fast, single-seat fighters to the approach of inbound bombers. Chennault was impressed by a British warning system that relied on ground observers in the preradar era. Setting his network in place for an Air Corps exercise at Fort Knox, Kentucky, in May 1933, Chennault verified the ability of a warning net to make timely inputs to fighter aviation assets, allowing successful intercepts of bomber formations.[73]

The prewar Air Corps did not embrace Chennault's philosophies in the main. Even as the Fort Knox exercise revealed merit in Chennault's thinking, another exercise in California prompted Air Corps Chief General Oscar Westover to declare that bombers could not be stopped. By 1937, Chennault's disappointment with the direction the Air Corps was taking accommodated his retirement on disability, followed by his employment by the Chinese government where Chennault established his view of pursuit aviation backed by a warning net.[74]

Echoing wording chosen by the British embassy in Washington, D.C., the British Military Attaché in Chungking, China, wrote to General Magruder in 1941, calling the AVG an "international air force." The British attaché urged that Chennault and his men be given whatever they needed to win their first battle, to set the tone of their war, saying the future of such a force as the AVG would depend largely upon the success Chennault could produce initially. According to a USAAF special study on the American Volunteer Group, the British attaché felt the Chinese "were incapable of operating and administering a modern air force; such a force would therefore have to be an international air force under international control."[75] (As the war evolved, Chinese pilots flew a variety of American-made fighters and bombers in combat.)

In fact, at this stage in 1941, the Chinese air force was in need of assistance quickly to stave off Japanese inroads. The only timely choice was the imposition of already skilled fighter pilots from other countries between the Chinese and the Japanese. Some literature made comparisons to the multi-national forces fighting in the Spanish civil war. In reality, this would be an American operation, albeit with newly released "civilian" pilots with recent American military experience.[76]

The American military attaché in Chungking told the War Department in August 1941 that Chennault envisioned having about 350 Americans organized by the middle of September, including 80 or 90 pilots. China's newly-furnished pursuit planes—Curtiss Tomahawk variants—would be organized by Chennault into three squadrons ready to wage war by the middle of October. As reported in the U.S. Army Air Forces study: "The American Volunteer Group was officially organized by the Chinese Government in October with Madame Chiang Kai-shek as the Honorary Commander. By October 15th it was far from ready for combat, although it was in training in Burma with 49 pilots. One hundred pilots had been hired, and the balance were enroute from the United States. However, even with their arrival, resignations and deaths would reduce the total to about 90." Concurrent with the buildup of the AVG in the fall of 1941, Generalissimo Chiang Kai-shek asked for American help in reorganizing the Chinese Air Force, in addition to the support he was receiving via the American-manned AVG. The impending invasion of Yunnan province by the Japanese spurred the Generalissimo's requests.[77]

By November 1941, the American Volunteer Group was in training in Burma. As the Burmese situation deteriorated under Japanese pressure, the British ambassador in Chungking vouched that a volunteer squadron of Brewster Buffalo fighters and one or two twin-engine Blenheim

Outdoor mechanics service a long-nose Tomahawk of the American Volunteer Group in China. *Air Force*

bombers were anticipated to be available to work with Chennault in Burma. Before America entered the war following the attack on Pearl Harbor, at least two plans were being bandied about regarding utilization of the AVG. One plan, to reinforce the AVG with American aviation units, was not favored by the Navy or the War Department. Another plan proposed inducting the AVG into the Army of the United States. As an Army Air Forces study noted: "The value of the (American Volunteer) Group lay more in its ability to draw the attention of the world to the struggle of China, than it did its actual combat efficiency. What military value it did possess would probably deteriorate rapidly under its chaotic organization. From the American angle, the only justification for induction was to correct the confused supply and maintenance system."[78]

If that assessment of the AVG by the wartime USAAF sounds like service rivalry, it is interesting to note how few of Chennault's pilots opted to stay with the group when it was absorbed into the USAAF during the war. Chaotic? Even after absorption into the USAAF, supplying units in China was no picnic.

The AVG's first mission came on 20 December 1941. Over the next eight months the Flying Tigers saw duty from airstrips at Kunming, Puoching, Hengyang, Kweilin, and Peishiyi in China, and Rangoon, Magwe, and Toungoo in Burma. During no time in its brief, yet storied career did the AVG have more than about 100 pilots. According to a subsequent wartime 23rd Fighter Group history, the average operational strength of the AVG was about 60 P-40s—mostly similar to B-models, with a few late-arriving P-40Es.[79] A core of obsolescent Curtiss Model 81A-2s, essentially P-40B-types, that had once been allocated to Sweden after the United States and Great Britain deemed them out of date, formed the basis of the AVG. These were the first aircraft to reach Burma for AVG training in September 1941.[80]

Chennault's original vision for the American Volunteer Group was to enter combat only after thorough training in the Far East, and never to commit his assets piecemeal, but to mass them for greatest effect. Japanese pressures on Burma rewrote the doctrine when the British there requested help, which came in the form of one of the AVG's three squadrons that was dispatched to Mingaladon on 12 December. In the next week,

General Chennault (at right of photo) posed with AVG members and a ceremonial flag in China. *Air Force Historical Research Agency*

the remaining two squadrons of Tomahawks moved east to Kunming to offer interceptor protection over the cities of southwest China, as well as to patrol the lifeline Burma Road. It was on 20 December 1941 that the Flying Tigers sank their teeth into Japanese bomber formations over Kunming, followed in three days over Rangoon, decimating the enemy. Chennault rotated his squadrons between Burma and China to even out the combat load on his fliers and planes. The men of the American Volunteer Group earned their fame, employing cool flying discipline and using the diving strengths of the Tomahawks to advantage against the Japanese aerial forces encountered. The lopsided aerial victories attributed to the AVG were due in part to the Flying Tigers' overriding will to fight on their own terms, using diving speed, and not engaging the more nimble Japanese fighters in turning engagements.[81]

As 1941 drew to a close, Chiang Kai-shek approved in principle the induction of the AVG into the Army of the United States, as the 23rd Pursuit Group, Interceptor. The Generalissimo and General Magruder diverged when it came to placement of the group, with Chiang Kai-shek not agreeing to sending the group or any part of it to Burma without his consent. The Generalissimo also insisted the new unit be placed under operational control of the Chinese High Command. Chiang Kai-shek prevailed on the basing of the Flying Tigers, after the U.S. War Department said the group was originally created for service to and in China, and therefore after induction into the Army of the United States its mission would remain the same. The Generalissimo could require the squadrons then flying over Burma to come back to China, with appropriate notification. The AAF study of the American Volunteer Group rather pointedly noted: "As a matter of record, even after the close of the Burma Road, and the consequent urgent need for fighting planes to protect the growing ferry line of transport planes over the Himalayan Hump which had to substitute for the Road, the War Department was of the same opinion."[82]

As January 1942 aged on the combat calendar, the momentum for inducting the AVG stagnated, and the Generalissimo and Madame Chiang Kai-shek seemed to some American observers to be less interested in that prospect. By the seventh day of March, Gen. "Vinegar" Joe Stilwell suggested to General Marshall that a personal message of appreciation from the U.S. Secretary of War to Chennault might speed up the process once more. The USAAF study noted: "Chennault knew that a large percentage of his pilots probably would not accept induction, and therefore recommended against the idea. He said that induction would utterly destroy the combat effectiveness of the (American Volunteer) Group and that it would take months to build up a force to take its place. By the end of March he was still of the opinion that the majority of his people would not favor induction."[83]

The uncertain direction of induction negotiations and the wearying grind of combat were wearing out the AVG's planes and men as casualties exacerbated a lack of replacement personnel, as well as spare parts for the Curtiss fighters. On 2 April 1942 General Stilwell, Captain Chennault, and Generalissimo Chiang Kai-shek reached an agreement on the mechanism for inducting the AVG, and picked the Fourth of July of that year for the transfer. Then, General Stilwell "turned his efforts toward insuring that the 10th Air Force maintain the combat effectiveness of the Group during the transition period," the AAF study reported. It was evident Chennault was right; many of his fabled AVG members would not be inducted, and President Roosevelt and Generalissimo and Madame Chiang Kai-shek sent personal appeals to the men of the AVG to stay until the change could be effected. According to the AAF study: "Captain Chennault knew his men well, and knew that in spite of all appeals, only a few would agree to induction and urged that replacements be rushed. In late May he predicted that even if replacements were furnished promptly, a new unit could not be tactically effective before the middle of September."[84]

Col. Robert Scott beams in the cockpit of a P-40K displaying his victory claims in China. *Air Force*

Both Chinese and American planners understood the significance of Chennault's contributions to the success and identity of the American Volunteer Group. Plans were formulated to keep Chennault in command of the unit after it became part of the AAF. Accordingly, Captain Chennault was recalled to active duty out of retirement on 9 April, and assigned to duty with the AVG. By the 22nd of April, he was promoted to colonel, and then nominated right away for promotion to brigadier general. The new Brig. Gen. Claire Chennault proposed, in June of 1942, that a new numbered air force be created for China since the 10th Air Force, headquartered in India, was too distant to effectively administer air units in China.[85] The idea did not take hold immediately, but the genesis of the 14th Air Force was in place.

General Chennault was given command of all American Air Forces in China, which remained under Chiang Kai-shek's control until the 4 July 1942 induction date for the AVG. After that date, U.S. military channels would prevail, with Chennault ultimately becoming first commander of the 14th Air Force in China when it was created in 1943.

By May of 1942, with the interceptor mission of the AVG largely preempted by ground attack sorties, and with no personnel replacements showing up since early December 1941, morale slumped, according to one USAAF account.[86] By this time, all three squadrons were in China, where Chennault tried to use them against air forces in protection of Chinese cities when possible. The Burma Road was useless and Rangoon was a shambles as Japan rampaged in Burma. General Stilwell commended the AVG for what it had accomplished as he tried to elevate the need for more men and materials to stop the Group's hemorrhaging. On 14 June 1942, a board of officers led by Chennault was appointed to induct qualified AVG members into U.S. service, and transfer equipment of the AVG to the U.S. Army. The U.S. government agreed to compensate China for equipment originally purchased by China, and to cancel charges for any Lend-Lease equipment that was transferred back to U.S. control. At that time, AVG strength was about 200; about 67 of this number were pilots and staff. When induction ceremonies were held in Kunming, China, only four qualified pilots opted to move with the American Volunteer Group into USAAF service. Chennault's forecast was correct—his Flying Tigers had no desire to rejoin the conventional American Air Force. Some, like Marine flier Greg Boyington, returned to their original branch of service rather than join the AAF. In all, 41 members of the AVG, in all positions, were inducted. To ease the transition into the 23rd Pursuit Group, 16 AVG pilots and 19 technicians volunteered to remain for two weeks following the disbanding of the AVG.[87]

The U.S. military mission to China printed conditions of induction for the AVG that included a provision for Chinese personnel who wanted to join the 23rd Pursuit Group: "Qualified Chinese pilots, technicians and other personnel may be commissioned or enlisted in the 23rd Pursuit Group of the United States Armed Forces for service outside the United States in accordance with U.S. Army regulations under the same conditions of service as American personnel, thereby showing to the world a true spirit of mutual cooperation and consolidation of the democratic front."[88]

The USAAF interviewed AVG pilots and mechanics several times in 1942, gathering this material into a file labeled "Information on Tactics of A.V.G.," dated 27 August 1942, using the slang and jargon of that wartime era. Included was a study on AVG fighter tactics that listed two types of fundamentals: "(1) Simple rules that are universal and should become second nature to all fighter pilots. (2) Tactics employed when using P-40s against Japanese fighters of superior maneuverability." In the latter category, the study urged P-40 pilots confronted by Japanese fighters of superior maneuverability: "Never use climbing maneuvers unless you have excess speed from a dive, because the Jap plane can outclimb you." Instead, P-40 fliers were told to "Use P-40's best characteristics; namely—speed, diving, and fire power (head-on runs). Never use maneuverability. Avoid aerobatics because the Jap planes can do them faster and in much less space. Never dogfight them."[89]

The tactics study extolled the values of altitude to P-40 pilots: "Altitude is good life insurance. If the enemy has two or three thousand feet altitude advantage on you, turn at right angles to his course, or even directly away from him, and

The British Tomahawk IIA (Curtiss Model H-81-A2), similar to the aircraft released for use by the American Volunteer Group. *Curtiss via Peter M. Bowers*

avoid him until you have enough distance to climb safely (to) at least his altitude. Climbing straight up into an enemy formation at 150 m.p.h. is almost a sure way to lose pilots and equipment." The study urged patience in P-40 pilots, waiting for an altitude advantage before diving to attack. Grimly, the study advised pilots who had to bail out in the vicinity of the enemy to wait as long as possible before opening the parachute, to avoid being machine-gunned on the way to the ground.[90]

Flying Tigers C. W. Sawyer, Robert Layher, and Robert Smith prepared a report on AVG experiences for the benefit of the 10th Air Force, under date of 2 May 1942. These three Tigers credited Claire Chennault with briefing tactics that worked in the skies over China and Burma. Teamwork was stressed, and the force of P-40s put aloft was earmarked with assault, support, and reserve elements to assist damaged P-40s. "It is practically suicide to drop out of a fight and try to struggle home with a crippled plane at low altitude," the report noted.[91]

Almost dispassionately, the three AVG fliers described typical enemy air operations: "Japanese tactics in our area have generally remained the same, with occasional minor changes, but we usually know what to expect after the first engagements. The very few times bombers came over without fighter escort, they always dropped their bombs and turned toward home upon sight of our fighters, regardless of how few there were of us. They went into a shallow dive and as a result of their speed were difficult to overtake. We would have to use full power in order to make repeated attacks and still stay with them."[92]

The report chronicled Japanese air discipline that caused the bombers to maintain close formation throughout an attack by the AVG: "The first raid we had was in China when 10 '97s' came over, dropped their bombs, when they sighted our fighters and turned tail for home. Although 8 of the 10 were shot down they never once lost their formation but kept filling in as the planes were shot out of the formation. Nor did they fly into any clouds which on this particular day were solid at 15,000 feet. They flew close to the top layer, but never through them, thus making it possible to make an attack, duck into the clouds and right out for another attack."[93]

In the face of unescorted Japanese bombers, the AVG often found it advantageous to parcel out its P-40s into at least three parts, the report explained: "If a head-on run was possible, make it in a somewhat 'line abreast' formation. After passing beneath the formation the center section does an Immelman if possible, and the outer section(s) chandelle up and to the side of the flanks, thus getting the force into position to make attacks from three directions at the same time. We used this method because it keeps the top gunners from concentrating their fire in any one direction. The sections on the flanks might make only feint attacks at first, keeping at long range and using only .50-caliber guns to draw the fire while the center section went in for close range fire, usually killing some of the gunners, after which everyone could come into close range with less return fire from the bombers. We tried to time all our attacks so as to all go in at the same time and from as many directions as possible, and keep firing until a break-away was necessary in order to avoid collision, the fire being concentrated on the engines and gas tanks area. We always tried to keep at least one plane over the fight to warn us of enemy fighters that might appear."[94]

A different scenario attended AVG air battles over Rangoon and central and northern Burma, the report said, where large formations of bombers were escorted by many fighters, with the fighters dispersed ahead, above, below, on both sides, and behind the bombers. "Due to the fact that we had only a small number of fighters to attack with," the report explained, "it was usually very hard for anyone to make a run on the bombers without picking up a bunch of enemy fighters on his tail. Therefore it was necessary to engage the fighters first, the(n) try to get at the bombers later when the fighters were more scattered. A large number of bombers were shot down after they had turned and headed for their bases."[95]

Japanese fighter sweeps presented their own problems for the Flying Tigers, the report noted: "Several times they would send over 50–75 fighters with no bombers. Against these the group would try to meet them head-on, and go straight through to break them up. The enemy fighters would then start using the 'flying circus' tactics. They would be stacked six to seven thousand feet, all doing a series of 'wing-overs' and in a circle of two (to) three miles in diameter. It looks like a bee-hive. When one of us got into it, 10–15 Japs would immediately be on his tail and all he could do was to roll or push over, and dam [sic] quick, then dive through the entire bunch, down and out, then come back for another pass. When we would make a run on an enemy fighter, and didn't get him, we had to leave him because even if you didn't pick up a bunch on your tail, and tried to follow him around for another burst, he would immediately turn inside you and be sitting on your tail himself. Therefore we used 'hit and run' tactics against fighters entirely. If we had the rare opportunity of being above them and were certain no more were above us we could sometimes attack and then pull up into the sun or clouds. The Jap would never follow us through clouds."[96]

The report contained a succinct summary recommendation from the three AVG fliers: "Pick your fight. You can carry the fight to him if you will just be patient at the beginning and use the clouds, sun, and wait till you have an altitude advantage. If you have to dive away from a fight it will take you 20 minutes to get into it again. If you have initial altitude advantage, you can dive, fire and climb again to repeat at very close intervals, thus doing much more damage and causing a great harassing effect."[97]

A terse potpourri of information gleaned in an interview of AVG pilots Kenneth Jernstedt, Charles Older, Robert Brouk, and John Farrell, printed 11 July 1942, included the following:

- "When attacking a Jap bomber don't dive too far before breaking off the attack. New pilots will learn this after their first pass; it is not a habit-forming mistake."
- "Don't hold a burst too long. One AVG came back with all six barrels bent because of this." (Aircraft M-2 .50-caliber machine guns used lightweight barrels that could become misshapen from the heat of prolonged firing.)
- "P-40 used for reconnaissance by cutting hole in bottom of baggage compartment and mounting camera with trigger in cockpit. All guns stripped except .50 cal." (This suggests a P-40B Tomahawk, which had mixed .30- and .50-caliber weapons, was used for the recce bird as opposed to the P-40E which used only .50-caliber guns.)

Chinese roundels and a sharkmouth, bisected by the fuselage camouflage demarcation, herald one of Chennault's Flying Tigers in China. *Bowers collection*

- "P-40 used for evacuation of personnel. One passenger sits in seat, pilot in his lap, other passenger in baggage compartment."[98]

Flying Tiger pilot George L. Paxton was credited in an AAF interview with a pithy recounting of Chennault's advice on the P-40, "In the first place, Chennault told us that we had a sorry airplane, as fighters go; that it had two things: (1) Diving speed and (2) Gun fire. If we used those, we could get by with them. If not, we were going to get shot up—cold turkey."[99]

The Paxton interview continued: "We flew a two-plane formation. Chennault told us to stick with our leader. We found an attack from quarter rear effective, by starting above (the) plane and diving down—a high four or five o'clock dive about 2,000 feet and come up and shoot. As you come up, he will have gone ahead over you, and you would have very little deflection. However, you don't want to get in that position until you are ready to shoot. That was the best way we found of getting bombers." Paxton's interview also described attacking bombers first that were on the extreme outside edge of a formation. "Don't go inside that cone of fire. We had two men lost that way—trying to come in on the leader of the Jap formation." Paxton's interview argued against spending prolonged time behind the Japanese bombers: "Some losses (to the AVG) were sustained from being sucked in directly behind. Use deflection for protection until you get ready to shoot. Then it would be simply a momentary thing—get your burst and then pull out. Their gunner would only have time for a very short burst at you."[100]

Paxton was quoted with eloquence in describing Chennault: "General Chennault has a marvelous knowledge for the work—knows airports; distances, in time, not miles—how long it takes a P-40 or B-25 to get there; knows when to send fighters in. He has a good general picture as to how Japs will move and what they are going to do." When the interviewer commented that men of the AVG "think quite a bit of the General, don't you," Paxton's response was said to be, "Yes, I especially. I think he is the finest man who ever lived."

Identified in a combat report excerpt only as "flight leader Greene" (possibly P. J. Greene), an AVG pilot described his harrowing encounter with a Japanese force of 50 bombers and fighters south of Rangoon on 23 December 1941: "After I had made four or five passes at the bombers, I noticed fighters coming down from behind. I then dropped back alone and engaged too many of them, firing at one Type 96 fighter from approximately 300 yards and saw him start down. Did not see him crash, but witnesses on ground did." Greene is further quoted: "I fired at another from point blank range who had just half-rolled and started down. Although I hit him plenty, I did not see him fall, for about this time there were fighters firing at me and evidently hit the controls, for the ship went completely out of control."[101]

"I bailed out and opened my chute too soon," the report quoted Greene as saying. "Was probably at 7,000 or 8,000 feet. One Japanese ship made one pass at chute and gave a long burst at me. He left and then another Japanese cut his motor and fired at me down to around 2,000 feet. All bullets missed me but several hit my chute. I landed in a rice field and was picked up by a British officer who took me to the hospital for first aid," Greene reported. After that, he returned to Mingaladon Aerodrome.[102]

A brief description of an AVG ground attack on a Japanese-held airfield on 9 January 1942, preserved in an AAF wartime document, said four P-40s of the American Volunteer Group took off at 11 A.M., flying to attack the airfield at Meshot, Burma, by noon. "Six planes spotted in line were set on fire during the first three runs—the other planes were no doubt damaged, but did not burn at once," the description said. Eight planes on the ground were burned, two were damaged, and one of the attacking P-40s was missing, while two other P-40s in the fight sustained bullet holes. After several attacking passes on the flightline, a fifth pass made by at least one of the P-40s targeted tents bordering the field, raking them with two .30-caliber machine guns. The Flying Tigers returned to base by 1:30 P.M.[103]

An interview by the USAAF with AVG mechanic W. W. Pentecost illuminated some aspects of life and operations with the Flying Tigers: "I made it a point to install new engines in planes wherever possible. The ships were shot down, and putting in new engines did give the boys a little bit of a break. In the field, we had to patch bullet holes and tears with adhesive tape.

Iron ring-and-bead gunsight components are visible on the cowling of this AVG Tomahawk. Splayed cooling gills on the underside of the fuselage ahead of the wing junction are open in the photo to promote engine cooling—a problem for liquid-cooled aircraft while on the ground. *Bowers collection*

We flew ships with several holes in the propeller blades. We had to get them into the air, as they were safer there than on the ground during raids." To keep the P-40s in commission, Pentecost is quoted in the interview as saying, "Repair work was done in the field at night to make the ships available for duty next morning. That was the answer to our success—we kept the ships flying in every possible way."[104]

Pentecost's interview included a discussion of structural failures in Japanese aircraft. The interviewer and Pentecost both are quoted as using the term "Zero" to describe the enemy aircraft; a fairly common habit early in the war of calling any Japanese fighter a "Zero" may obscure the actual planes involved, but the gist of the anecdote remains the same: "A favorite maneuver is to dive the P-40s steeply with the Zeros on your tail—dive about 5,000 feet and pull out as rapidly as you can. The Zero will keep right on going. I have seen them shed everything—wings, tail surfaces, even the pilot. Their (Japanese aircraft) construction is very flimsy and not to be compared with American ships. Riveting and skin surfaces are good, but the structural frame is not."[105] (Whatever other aircraft the Flying Tigers may have encountered, the AVG definitely faced Nakajima Ki.43 Hayabusas, called "Oscar" by the Allies. Oscars enjoyed a maneuvering advantage over the P-40, and this credible Nakajima fighter has long been in the shadow of the more famous Zero.)

Pentecost's interview included comments about P-40 field maintenance, and what could be done to improve interchangeability, "We were able to interchange ailerons, rudders, and sometimes whole panels. Wings were interchanged several times, but usually required refitting. Fairings gave us the most trouble. Almost always the holes for fastenings had to be slotted, and sometimes redrilled to make the fairing fit."[106] At this early time, with prewar Tomahawks, the manufacture of aircraft was still a hand-fit process in many areas, in spite of mass production techniques and theory.

Frank G. Metasavage, an AVG mechanic, was interviewed by the USAAF in 1942. His descriptions of life on the flightline included, in the

AVG P-40E, toting a long-finned bomb, has painted-out fuselage insignia since Chinese fighters did not use fuselage roundels at this time. The sharkmouth on this later Flying Tiger has a red and black interior added. *SDAM*

paraphrasing of the interviewer, the following, "The outfit was seriously handicapped in operations by lack of parts and tools and was only able to keep going because of consistent long hard hours of work by the mechanics. The pilots themselves performed some repairs on their own planes."[107]

Of the P-40s taken into the 23rd Fighter Group when the AVG was disbanded, some were still on hand over a year later. On 13 September 1943, the 23rd Fighter Group listed several P-40s, including the following ex-AVG aircraft, in need of retirement from combat service, due in part to the wear and tear listed since their acquisition by the 23rd Group:[108]

P-40E (41-36519), number 108, assigned to the 76th Fighter Squadron; had two engine changes and damaged in combat twice since assignment to the 23rd Fighter Group.

P-40E (41-36493), number 124, assigned to the 76th Fighter Squadron; had one engine change and damaged in combat twice.

P-40E (41-5698), number 159, assigned to the 75th Fighter Squadron; had one engine change and one serious groundloop accident.

P-40E (41-5706), number 180, assigned to the 75th Fighter Squadron; had two serious accidents and two wing changes due to "inherent instability of the plane in flight."

P-40E (41-36503), number 152, assigned to the 75th Fighter Squadron; belly-landed at Hengyang where it remained for two months; had sheetmetal work done twice; had a serious wheels-down accident at Chengkung; and had two engine changes.

P-40E (41-36524), number 153, assigned to the 75th Fighter Squadron; was shot up in combat twice and had landing gear change.

P-40E (41-36507), number 158, assigned to the 75th Fighter Squadron; was in local repair factory seven times (twice shot up in battle; one groundloop by crew chief; one taxiing accident; three serious landing mishaps).

The storied Flying Tigers are credited with a victory tally of 229 Japanese aircraft downed in flight and a further 69 destroyed on the ground for the loss of a dozen P-40s in combat and 61 on the ground.[109] With skill, courage, and discipline, the men of the American Volunteer Group used an inferior number of obsolescent fighters to wreak havoc in the skies over China and Burma in the darkest days of the Pacific war.

Tuskegee Airmen Demolished Barriers

To a generation of Americans, it is hard to imagine a segregated military: an Army Air Force in which blacks were routinely assigned to base custodial duties, often in "C" Squadron. (Some people at the time explained that the "C" meant Colored.) But the military merely reflected society. When pressure for social change was applied, one result was the establishment, even before American entry in World War II, of an Army Air Forces–sponsored primary flying training program for black men, at the Tuskegee Institute, not far from Montgomery, Alabama.

As war came to America, black fliers were trained by the USAAF in fighters as well as B-25s, although only the 332nd Fighter Group, preceded by its 99th Fighter Squadron, went into combat service. The 99th entered combat with P-40s in the Mediterranean, after learning on Warhawks in the United States.

The 332nd Group's manning was a varied mix of talents and ages, such as 50-year-old Second Lieutenant Alvin Williams who became adjutant for the Group's 100th Fighter Squadron; and Major Sam W. Westbrook Jr., a flier in civilian life, and a longtime member of the Army, who assumed command of the Group on 3 December 1942. The Group's morning report for 31 December 1942 showed a strength of 3 officers attached, 21 enlisted men "assigned," and 15 enlisted men (white) "attached."[110]

As 1942 drew to a close, the Group historian pondered problems unique to the fledgling black flying unit. Where would qualified blacks with USAAF specializations come from, if they were not currently being trained in AAF schools? The historian noted: "What was to be done with the 332nd Fighter Group was a question that only those in Washington could answer. Where were the pilot replacements coming from when they were only graduating at the rate of 8 to 10 pilots every six weeks? Where were the aircraft mechanics, . . . radio technicians, and various specialists coming from when there were none in training? These and many other factors must be solved the coming New Year." As January 1943 unfolded, the 332nd's historian noted, probably wryly, "At last the members of the 332nd Fighter Group have opened their own mess hall and were no longer a menace to the 318th Base and Air Base Squadron."[111]

By 29 March 1943, the 332nd Fighter Group had moved to Selfridge Field, Michigan, where a white fighter squadron, the 403rd, also under command of (by then) Lieutenant Colonel Sam Westbrook Jr., was activated "to function in a supervisory capacity in the training of the 332nd Fighter Group." Next month, portions of the Group moved farther north to Selfridge's sub-base at Oscoda, Michigan. The Group historian noted for April 1943, "The month of April signaled the beginning of intensive operational training of the 332nd Fighter Group composed of youthful Americans destined to make history for this country." On the 12th of April, the 332nd history noted, "The Group entertained 20 prominent Negro citizens (from the Detroit area) giving them a sample of Army life . . . while overhead a tight formation of P-40 Warhawks were going through their maneuvers." The visitors ranged from Dr. J. J. McClendon, president, and William Jackson, vice president, of the National Association for the Advancement of Colored People (NAACP) to Sonny Edwards, described in the unit history as a "free-lance photographer and deputy sheriff."[112]

During the summer of 1943, the 332nd continued to hone its skills at Selfridge and Oscoda. Early in the Group's association with Curtiss P-40s for stateside training, tired C-models handed down from First Air Force were used. The presence of characteristic sharkmouth motifs on some of these weary P-40s may have given rise to rumors the black fliers were using the remnants of the Flying Tigers, although painted teeth on P-40s had long before become a worldwide cliché. Elements of the 332nd temporarily replaced their P-40s with Bell P-39 Airacobras in September 1943, and there is some evidence to suggest the USAAF even considered equipping the black fliers with P-63 Kingcobras for combat.

In transition training near Tuskegee, Lieutenant Mac Ross underwent a chilling flight that garnered him some unsolicited "firsts" when his Merlin-powered P-40F began issuing smoke from its tight cowling. In the company of two other newly minted Tuskegee airmen, Lieutenant Ross tried gamely to return his ailing Warhawk to base, descending from 6,000 feet as the smoke continued to proliferate. Finally, at the urging of his formation mates, the lieutenant bailed out of the burning P-40 when it descended to an altitude of 3,000 feet. Lieutenant Ross thereby became the first black airman to survive the loss of his military aircraft in flight, as well as the first black eligible to join the Caterpillar Club for fliers whose lives had been saved by parachuting. He landed in a cotton field. Though exonerated of any error in the incident, Lieutenant Ross is said to have stewed for some time over it, fearful he might have set back the progress of black fliers in the AAF.[113]

The 99th Fighter Squadron preceded the rest of the 332nd Fighter Group into combat, over Pantelleria on 2 June 1943. This followed a tedious stateside waiting period of months with no movement orders forthcoming. Traveling from Tuskegee to Camp Shanks, New York, the 400

When a group of Tuskegee Airmen moved to Selfridge Field to continue training in P-40s, their armorers were photographed working on M-2 .50-caliber machine guns in July 1943. *Air Force photo*

After an aerial gunnery training mission in June 1943, Tuskegee fliers walked from their P-40s. From left to right: Lieutenants Edward C. Gleed, Peter Verwayne, Andrew Maples, Robert Diez, John H. Prowell, and William Griffin. *Air Force photo*

men of the 99th Fighter Squadron boarded a troop ship on 15 April 1943, sighting Africa nine days later, and disembarking at Casablanca. Initially stationed near Fez, the men of the 99th Squadron enjoyed cordial relations with other, white, AAF units there, engaging in impromptu contests between the black aviators' P-40s and the whites' A-36 variants of the Mustang. The men of the 99th ferried in their own brand-new P-40s—more than two dozen of them, probably all L- and F-models—from Casablanca. For the first time in their military flying careers, the men from Tuskegee had the luxury of new aircraft. Three white fighter pilots with combat seasoning were assigned to help break-in the fliers of the 99th in North Africa. Among these was Lieutenant Colonel Phillip Cochran, whose finesse in Warhawks in North Africa was by then the stuff of legend. By the end of May 1943, the 99th Fighter Squadron was attached to the white 33rd Fighter Group.[114]

Nose art and nicknames got off to a slow start on the P-40s of the 99th Fighter Squadron. The black aviators were for a time discouraged from adorning their Warhawks with any custom painting that might identify the flier inside. Concern was expressed over apparent German interest in the black airmen, and nobody was desirous of being singled out as a target.[115]

Mixed flights of, typically, six P-40s from the 33rd Fighter Group and two from the 99th Fighter Squadron were flown, with the first combat sorties by black AAF pilots occurring on 2 June 1943 in a strafing mission against targets on Pantelleria. During nine days of ground attacks against Pantelleria, the men of the 99th never flew less than 16 sorties a day. Ironically, the long stateside wait before receiving orders for overseas movement may have made the men from Tuskegee the best-trained new P-40 pilots to arrive in North Africa, for they had more training time than many whites who were sent out more quickly. A June 9 engagement with FW-190s escorting German bombers afforded the 99th Squadron its first taste of air-to-air combat, during which Lieutenant Willie Ashley damaged a Luftwaffe fighter, but could not verify its demise.[116]

The early sorties of the 99th Fighter Squadron were not without mishap; the first black pilot to drop a bomb in anger returned to base in North Africa only to taxi into an old bomb crater, damaging his Warhawk, and bruising this high-time P-40 flier's pride. Soon the 99th Squadron was realigned with the 324th Fighter Group, and relocated to the Cape Bon Peninsula to fly escort missions for bombers striking the western por-

Remnants of snow melt on the ramp in Michigan as men of the 332nd Fighter Group service P-40s in 1943. *Air Force photo*

tions of Sicily in the few days prior to Allied invasion there. The first such mission came on July 1; the next day, the 99th Fighter Squadron got its first confirmed victory when Lieutenant Charles B. Hall interposed his Merlin-powered P-40 between a pair of marauding FW-190s and the B-25s the 99th was assigned to protect. Lieutenant Hall got the angle on the German fighters in a turn, and fired a long burst, possibly borne of eagerness in his first aerial combat. Tracers poked the second FW-190 as he was in a left turn; then the German fighter dropped earthward rapidly, as the black lieutenant followed his plunge to a dusty conclusion. Hall, described as fearless, used the aging P-40 to run up a kill tally of three enemy aircraft before he rotated home, never getting the chance to try his skills in the faster Mustangs that later replaced the Warhawks.[117]

That second day of July also saw Tuskegee airman Lieutenant Walter Lawson attack a German aircraft for which he was given a "probable" victory. But the day was marked with a new kind of sadness for the fresh combat fliers, as two of their number, Lieutenants Sherman White and James McCullin, died as a result of groundfire hits their Warhawks took.

As the invasion of Sicily dominated MTO operations on 10 July 1943, Warhawks of the 99th Fighter Squadron bombed, strafed, and flew escort missions to further that objective. A scant nine days later, the first black fighter pilots in the USAAF flew their P-40s from Licata, Sicily, using real estate recently wrested from the Axis. Lieutenant Colonel Benjamin O. Davis Jr. returned from a stint with the 99th Squadron to assume command of the 332nd Fighter Group in October 1943. The debut of black combat fliers in the AAF received mixed reviews, with some white officers initially questioning the 99th's skill, and will. On the other side, the popular and populist war correspondent Ernie Pyle lauded the men from Tuskegee in his volume, *Brave Men*.

Even as they faced Axis fighters and anti-aircraft gunners in combat, the effectiveness of the men of the 99th Fighter Squadron came under question in some AAF spheres of influence. Accordingly, on 30 March 1944, the Statistical Control Division of the Office of Management Control filed a mathematically based comparison of the 99th Fighter Squadron's combat record and the record of other P-40 squadrons in the Mediterranean Theater of Operations. In early July 1943, the 99th Squadron flew mostly beach patrol sorties with some escort and bombing missions, not unlike other P-40 squadrons in the area, the report noted. In October, the 99th was attached to the 79th Fighter Group and moved to Foggia, where, until 16 January 1944, the squadron's P-40s were flown along the east coast of Italy, the statistical report noted, "in support of ground troops, its missions being mainly against gun positions, supply and ammunition stores, and shipping. No enemy aircraft were encountered during this period." Later that month, missions supported the Allies at Anzio.[118]

In comparing the 99th with P-40 squadrons manned by whites, the study did not include the 99th's early operations in June 1943. (Though not stated, it is possible this was done to give the 99th the benefit of the doubt for any early combat problems that might beset any brand-new unit. In fact, it has been argued that the 99th had a uniquely difficult baptism by fire because there were no previously seasoned black combat pilots to lead the young organization into battle.) But from July 1943 through the end of January 1944, the study noted:

- The 99th Fighter Squadron destroyed 12 enemy aircraft in combat, compared with an overall average of 9.8 for P-40 squadrons in the 12th Air Force. This was based on two hectic encounters, on January 27 and 28, when the 99th engaged a total of 38 German aircraft, claiming 12 destroyed, 2 probables, and 4 damaged; only 2 enemy aircraft had been encountered by the squadron in the previous half year, when it performed many beach patrol and bombing attacks.
- The 99th was slightly higher than the rest of 12th Air Force's P-40 squadrons in noneffective aircraft dispatched, at 8.51 percent versus 7.63 percent for the other P-40 units compared.
- The 99th Fighter Squadron flew the largest percentage of its missions in the study period (40.2 percent) on armed patrol and reconnaissance, compared with a percentage of 29.7 in that category for other 12th Air Force P-40 units; while the 99th flew objective bombing missions 38.9 percent of the time, other 12th Air Force P-40 squadrons devoted 50.8 percent of their missions to objective bombing. Other mission profiles (escort, strafing, and other) had variations less than 2 percent between the 99th and the other P-40 squadrons of 12th Air Force.[119]

Part of the study tried to correlate where the 99th's planes were on days when other P-40 units in 12th Air Force encountered enemy fighters. The list of missions for the 99th between 20 July and 17 September 1943 includes continuous patrols over Joss Beach from 5:30 A.M. to 8:39 P.M.

Lieutenant Colonel Benjamin O. Davis Jr., assumed command of the 332nd Fighter Group 8 October 1943. *Air Force photo*

An early short-bodied P-40F seen from above reveals the smooth nose contour of Merlin-engined Warhawks. Both elevators have trim tabs, but only the left wing's aileron has a tab. Radio antenna wires stretch from each horizontal stabilizer to a dorsal fuselage location. *AAF via Bowers collection*

on July 21; bombing strikes on the Cesaro-Randazo Road on July 28; more beach patrols and transportation attacks in July and August; and bomber escort to Salerno on September 16 and 17, including escorting B-25s on the second date.[120] (Subsequently, the 332nd would equip with P-51s and establish a reputation for diligent bomber escort missions, including a 24 March 1945 mission over Berlin during which the men of the 332nd bagged three German jet fighters.)[121]

If it is unsettling to contemplate statistical analyses of combat pilots in the USAAF based on race, it would be well to remember that the fliers from Tuskegee distinguished themselves in combat and broke new ground. The struggles of the first black USAAF fliers over a half century ago do not reflect any heightened bias in the Army Air Forces at that time; rather, it is a reflection of society at that time, and how times have changed.

In October 1943, the 99th Fighter Squadron was placed with the white 79th Fighter Group at Foggia, Italy. It was a fortuitous assignment, as the black fliers soon learned to appreciate the managerial acumen of 79th Fighter Group commander Colonel Earl Bates, who truly integrated operations of the 99th with those of the other Warhawk squadrons. Standout comparisons became impossible to make as everyone flew the same missions. The men of the 99th gained ever more experience and insight from their relationship with seasoned fliers in the 79th Group. It was a time for accomplishment by the fliers of the 99th. With Allied troops engaged in a serious fight at Anzio in early 1944, the pilots of the 99th found opportunities, on January 27 and 28, to rack up 12 more aerial victories, some over the embattled Anzio beachhead. Four more victories accrued to the men of the 99th while flying Warhawks over Italy in February 1944. Later that spring, the 99th Fighter Squadron was reassigned successively to two other groups. By early July 1944, the combat-wise 99th was assigned to the unique black 332nd Fighter Group in Italy, and the durable Merlin-powered Warhawks were turned in for North American P-51 Mustangs.

While other ethnic minorities from America also distinguished themselves in a variety of combat heroics during World War II, perhaps none had to overcome the degree of social prejudice from the white community that initially clung to the black flier program like parasitic drag to an airframe. If, in hindsight, the right of all Americans to compete for pilot positions seems too obvious, too simple, don't use that hindsight to diminish the fortitude of the men who stuck it out with the 99th Fighter Squadron and the 332nd Fighter Group, thereby teaching us all something about patriotism and patience.

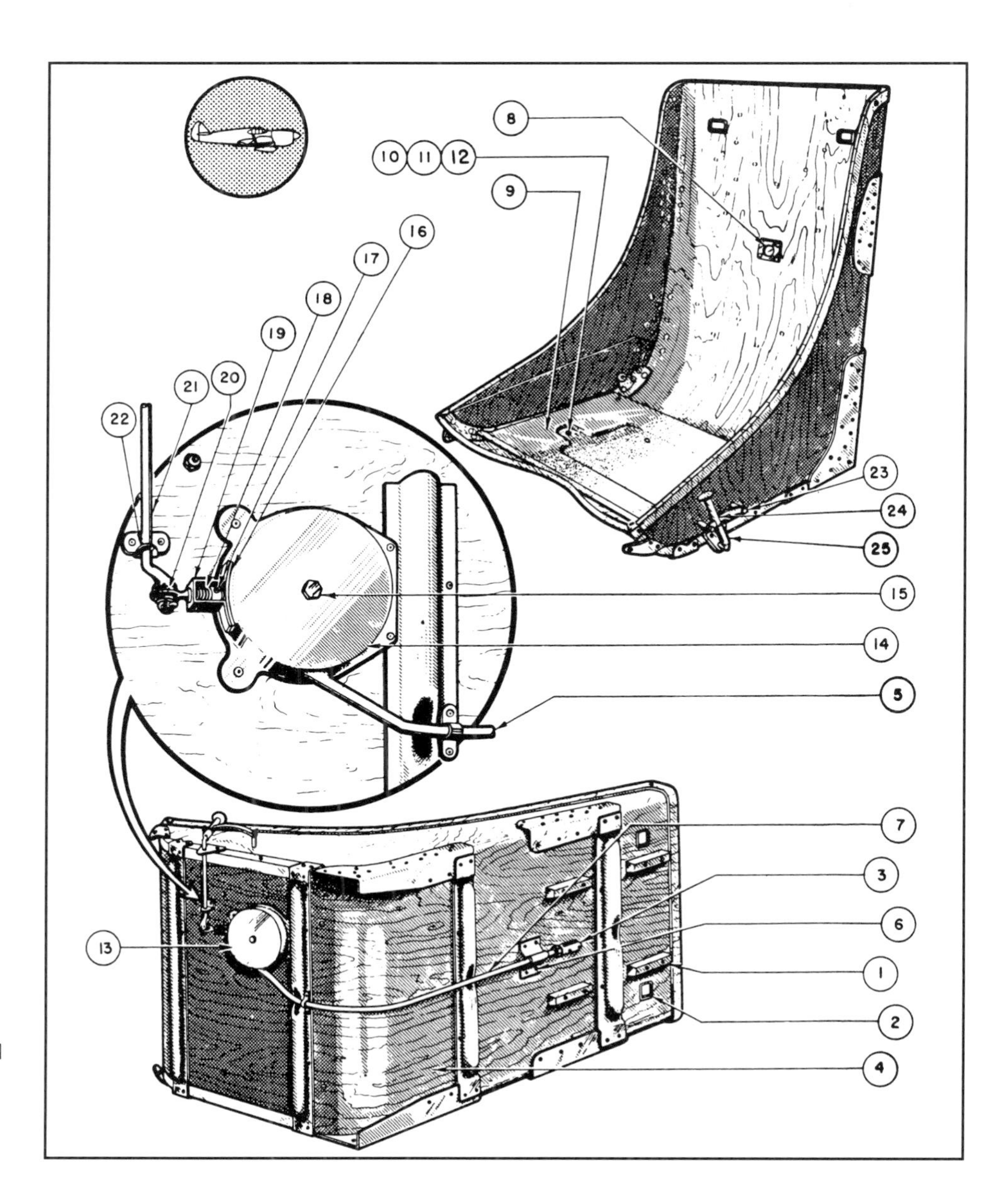

As depicted in a Warhawk illustrated parts manual, some P-40s were equipped with molded wooden pilot seats in an effort to conserve metal. *Wayne Fiamengo collection*

P-40s Against a Rising Sun

The following vignettes illuminate aspects of the P-40's war in the Pacific—aspects that sometimes are overlooked by some who presume the vast areas of the Pacific war were somehow less important than the European conflict. Tell that to the men who fought the rays of the rising sun of Japan in their durable P-40s.

Early Challenge from Yanks Down Under

Hindsight robs us of the desperate sense of urgency faced by American fliers in the Philippines, Java, and Australia in the first month of war, for we *know* how it is going to turn out; they could only guess and have faith. As General

Perhaps the last peacetime photo these P-40 pilots posed for, this group portrait at Wheeler Field on 1 December 1941 features (left to right): First Lieutenant W. L. Hayes, Headquarters Squadron; Major A. W. Tyler, 45th Pursuit Squadron commander; Major P. W. Blanchard, Jr., 15th Pursuit Group commander; Major G. H. Austin, 47th Pursuit Squadron commander; First Lieutenant L. M. Sanders, 46th Pursuit Squadron commander. *Air Force*

A Royal Australian Air Force Kittyhawk IV in New Guinea has been armed with a pair of underwing bombs, with a provision for a third bomb or gas tank on the centerline of the fuselage. White paint on the leading edge of the wing, and on tail, was a southwest Pacific theater marking. *Sommerich via Bowers*

Brereton mustered his resources in the face of advancing Japanese forces, he ordered on 14 January 1942 the creation of the 17th Pursuit Squadron (Provisional) under Major Charles A. Sprague. The major was to mold men and airplanes then on hand at Amberley Field in Brisbane, Australia, into his fighting force. The presence of 17 combat-ready P-40Es dictated the squadron's initial complement of fighters, matched by a like number of pilots. To this were added 17 crew chiefs and 17 armorers, plus a first sergeant, a line chief, and three radio men. Pilots with recent combat led new fliers fresh from California's Hamilton Field.[122]

The 17 P-40Es left Brisbane in two formations the morning of January 16. Major Sprague led the first nine Curtisses, escorted by a twin Beech. Lieutenant Walter Coss headed up the second flight of the remaining eight P-40s, accompanied by a pair of Fairey Battle escorts—it was common to use aircraft with superior navigational facilities to guide gaggles of single-seat fighters across the trackless Pacific. The first stopover did not bode well for the resource-strained squadron when Lieutenant Carl Geis' P-40 groundlooped at the end of the Rockhampton runway following an electrical failure that robbed him of the use of flaps, brakes, and propeller pitch control. Both flights continued to their overnight destination of Townsville, where another P-40 washed out in a landing accident. After a third incident, the number of 17th Squadron P-40s finally reaching Darwin on January 17 and 18 was down to 14 aircraft.[123]

Tropical enemies came in many guises, and while awaiting further orders at Darwin in January, one of the pilots exhibited the pain and fever of dengue, a contagious disease that forced him to stay behind when the rest of the squadron departed for Timor on January 22. Captain Gunn escorted the P-40s with the twin Beech, crossing 540 miles of open water without incident. But the attrition before combat was not over; at Koepang, Timor, another pilot contracted dengue fever. He and his P-40 remained behind as the rest of the unit proceeded to its destination of Soerabaja, Java, by way of Waingapoe between January 22 and 24. On January 24, the P-40 waiting at Timor with its incapacitated pilot was destroyed in a Japanese air raid. At Java, only 12 P-40Es were in commission; a 13th would be added to the roster. Dutch military forces at Soerabaja worked with the P-40 fliers, and on January 26, in inclement weather, 6 P-40s flew a coastal patrol and flew cover for a damaged Dutch submarine until deteriorating skies forced a recall of the fighters to Soerabaja. Upon landing, Lieutenant Frank Neri cracked up his P-40.[124]

Now clearly down to 12 P-40s and 13 pilots, the 17th engaged in flights to identify aircraft in the vicinity. Time was spent maintaining and repairing the P-40Es, but sparse numbers of mechanics and a lack of complete spares hindered business already. The air war came calling on the 17th Provisional Squadron on 3 February 1942 at 10:45 in the morning when Japanese bombers made their first incursion over Java. With about 20 to 25 minutes' advance warning, the P-40s were unable to reach the attackers before they dropped their bombs, but the Warhawks of the 17th rose to intercept the Japanese force at 21,000 feet, north of Soerabaja. Four of the fighters made contact with the bomber force of 17 aircraft, giving chase for 85 miles out to sea as the Warhawks closed the gap and ran low on gasoline. Two of the American pursuits had to abandon the chase for lack of fuel; the other two each made one earnest stern attack,

A simple cockpit array, sturdy rudder pedal mounts, and a large curved windscreen glazing of laminated safety glass are evident in this P-40F. *Bowers collection*

To ease new pilots into the Warhawk, TP-40N two-seaters were developed. The track for the aft canopy extends over the national insignia. *Curtiss via Peter M. Bowers*

and one Warhawk pilot claimed one Japanese Type 96 bomber shot down.[125]

In the hectic early months of the Pacific war, identification of Japanese warplanes was sometimes less than scientific, and in need of codification. With several Type 96s in Japanese service, the bomber claimed that day over Java was almost certainly a Mitsubishi G3M Navy Type 96 twin-engine attack bomber. When two of the P-40s made contact with a Japanese fighter force that morning about 80 miles south of Soerabaja, the American fliers reported seeing Zeros and "long range Seversky fighters," according to a squadron report. While the Japanese Navy had purchased 20 Seversky two-seat 2PA-B3 fighters, which saw service in the Sino-Japanese war of the 1930s, it is believed these were phased out by the time of the Java action in 1942.[126]

The two P-40 pilots made a two-ship formation attack against six of the Japanese fighters. If those odds weren't bad enough, the young Americans were then bounced from behind and above by more fighters that mortally struck the P-40E flown by Lieutenant James Rowland, whose crash made him the 17th's first combat death. Lieutenant Coss, alone in a wilderness of enemy fighters, attacked again, claiming one shot down. (He identified it as one of the so-called Severskys.) As Warhawks of the 17th Squadron recovered (in what a contemporary squadron report called "extremely mucky weather") at their newly finished airstrip at Blimbing (sometimes referred to as Ngoro), they could now muster only 11 P-40s and a dozen pilots.

Three P-40Es—remnants of a force of 10 that was hacked up on the ground by a Japanese raid on Bali—landed at Soerabaja in early February. Two were immediately absorbed into the struggling 17th Squadron; one remained at Soerabaja for repairs to damage suffered in combat. But the give-and-take of wartime conditions had a debit column, and on February 6, a U.S. Marine Corps aviator took off in one of the P-40s. Engine trouble plagued his landing, and he was killed in the ensuing crash. "He was buried on the same day at Blimbing," a squadron report noted tersely. Identified in squadron accounts as Captain Reed, the ill-fated Marine had been an aviation instructor working with the Dutch. Dutch Air Defense Command (ADC) came in for some criticism by the P-40 pilots when they were directed to chase sup-

Mechanics in training learn the core of Warhawk engine operation and maintenance at a Curtiss P-40 school on 24 February 1943. *Air Force*

posed Japanese formations that could not be found, or were eventually confirmed as Allied in origin. On February 7, after a tail-chasing adventure, the 17th noted in a report: "ADC . . . misdirected the movement of the squadron and kept us chasing ourselves." Good news that day came in the form of a baker's dozen Warhawks that flew in to Blimbing to boost squadron strength to 22 aircraft. When one P-40 washed out on landing that day, the day's report listed 21 Warhawks in the squadron; 20 at Ngoro and 1 at Soerabaja. Sixteen were ready and available for combat.[127]

The apparent misidentification of Japanese warplanes led to a claim in the first week of February that the 17th Fighter Squadron had shot down a presumably Japanese-operated Messerschmitt Me-110 twin-engine fighter, which the 17th called a "reconnaissance bomber." (Japanese aircraft historian Rene Francillon says no Me-110s were actually used by the Japanese, but the rumor of their presence in the Pacific even led to the assigning of a code name—Doc—to the type presumed for a while to be in Japanese combat service.)

The squadron got a crack at another Japanese bomber force on February 9, but the climb to interception altitude at 24,000 feet strung the 15 American fighter pilots out, and subsequently only five of the fliers accurately copied the sighting of the Japanese bombers by Lieutenant Roger Williams. The 5 Warhawks waded into 18 bombers split into two flights of 9 apiece. The humid air over Java was cleft by knifing P-40Es zipping out strings of copper-jacketed .50-caliber bullets toward the Japanese bombers. All of the Warhawk pilots executed at least one attack against the bombers; the persistence of one of their number, making four runs at the enemy, led to observations of one Japanese bomber momen-

Methods of extending fighter range received attention at home and abroad. In August 1942, P-40E-1 (41-25094) was used in the United States to evaluate a nonmetallic centerline 150-gallon gas tank, which used a streamlined fairing to seal the gap between the tank and the fuselage. Another test configuration used a pair of wide 225-gallon tanks. *Bowers collection*

tarily issuing smoke from its left engine. When ADC subsequently logged the crash of a Japanese bomber that morning, the 17th Fighter Squadron pilot who pressed home four attacks received credit for the kill, said to be the squadron's second Type 96. Along the way, 3 Zeros also were added to the squadron tally.[128]

A few P-40Es continued to trickle in to the squadron to bolster Java operations, often at a price of a few aircraft wrecked for a greater number taken on strength in the same transaction. And normal attrition picked away at the roster; on February 12 and 15, landing accidents, one on a wet runway, claimed 2 of the P-40Es, after which the squadron could tally 30 Warhawks on strength.

The Warhawks of 1942 could shackle a total of six small (usually 20- or 30-pound) bombs under their wings. The 17th Pursuit Squadron made ready to go on the offensive with diminutive bomb loads of four apiece on February 17.[129] Squadron skipper Major Sprague led eight P-40s staging from Batavia, over the Java Sea in moderate weather, intent on dive-bombing and strafing Palembang, Sumatra. In the morning light, six Japanese fighters (identified by the Warhawk pilots as 97 Series—probably meaning Nakajima Ki-27 Army Type 97 fighters) jumped the bomb-laden P-40Es. It must have been a deadly annoyance to the Americans, for the Type 97s, with their fixed landing gear and under-300-miles per hour top speeds were no match for P-40Es, but half the American flight jettisoned their bombs to better maneuver in engaging the Japanese intercepting force. Four P-40 pilots each claimed a Japanese fighter downed in that encounter. The three Warhawks still retaining their small bombs dive-bombed as planned, with one of the P-40s going after barges on the river with bombs and guns. By 8:30 that morning, the first of the returning P-40s announced its landing approach back at Batavia with the clatter of exhaust reports as the throttle was reduced. In a commendable bout of modesty and accuracy, the 17th Pursuit Squadron noted in a contemporary report, "ADC at Soerabaja had given the squadron credit for considerably more victories than claimed by the pilots."[130] And so goes one of the difficult processes for historians of the Second World War, especially when dealing with the turbulent early months in the Pacific—tallies of enemy planes shot down are sometimes suspect. What remains, after the claims are discounted or proven, is the undeniable ledger showing young Americans pitting themselves and their rapidly aging P-40s in mortal combat with an advancing enemy of unknown strength.

The squadron was busy on February 19 and 20, discouraging Japanese bombers over Java and escorting LB-30s and A-24s on bombing runs over Bali. When the smoke of battle cleared on the 20th, among four missing P-40 pilots was squadron commander Major Sprague. Even as 17th Pursuit Squadron strength increased, so did the seemingly unstoppable momentum of the Japanese. The 17th Squadron reported hectic activity on February 21: "Four flights of the squadron were ordered in the air by ADC and contacted the enemy at 20,000 feet over Soerabaja. A and B flights were attacked from above by enemy Zero fighters. There were quite a few actual dogfights engaged in, but most P-40s were forced to dive away. Lieutenant Hynes was shot down and killed during this engagement. C and D flights contacted enemy bombers below them and were able to make one attack individually. More Zero fighters attacked them from the rear and above, and they were forced to dive out. During this contact Lieutenant Hoskyns was shot down and killed." The men of the 17th Pursuit Squadron were learning to apply the first lesson of combat with Zeros: Don't dogfight; dive away to fight again in quick passes at high speed. The squadron believed it accounted for four Zeros that day; ADC added two bombers to the tally of credits. Squadron P-40 strength had ebbed to 18 aircraft total, with only 17 in commission.[131]

With Major Sprague missing in action, command of the squadron passed to Captain Grant Mahoney; his subsequent temporary departure at the behest of General Brereton left Lieutenant Joseph L. McCallum in command of a beleaguered combat unit on February 24. The din of battle has no emotion except that with which we animate it. The blunt reality of combat the very next day saw Lieutenant McCallum bail out of his stricken P-40E after being bounced by Zeros at about 26,000 feet over Soerabaja. The 17th recorded what happened, "ADC informed the squadron that he had been machine-gunned in his parachute and was dead." Whether true or

In March 1945, this P-40K-5 (42-9873) was photographed at Barrackpore, Calcutta. A crudely repainted serial on the rudder omitted the digit "2," which signified the fiscal year the aircraft was ordered. *Peter M. Bowers*

rumor, if this story about a vulnerable flier hanging in his 'chute harness was retold throughout the Pacific, it no doubt embittered Allied fliers. Fifty-four Japanese bombers, plus perhaps 36 fighter escorts, had stormed over Java that day; after the air-to-air combat, the 17th Pursuit Squadron was tapped to reconnoiter Baween Island, north of Soerabaja, to search for a rumored Japanese invasion fleet. Java was threatened.

Like birds moving inland to avoid a tropical storm, six Dutch Brewster Buffalo fighters and an equal number of Hurricane fighters piloted by Dutch fliers arrived at the 17th Pursuit Squadron's airfield to bolster strength for the next round of Java air battles. Japanese raids continued, sometimes too high for effective interception in time by the P-40s and Brewsters. A 17th Pursuit Squadron report noted: "Many P-40s were being forced to return to the field because of motor trouble. The planes had about 150 hours of combat time put on them with little or no maintenance. All ships were forced to remain on alert all day, and this work could not be done." The surging power needs of combat could cause the sturdy Allison engines to be run at high settings where any powerplant would soon show the ravages of use.[132]

The men of the 17th received orders the night of 28 February 1942 to execute a raid the following dawn on the beach at Rembang, Java, to strafe the Japanese invasion force there, as well as ships offshore. "The mission was to be performed by all available P-40s, four Brewsters and six Hurricanes," a squadron report explained. "Plans were formulated to attack first with the P-40s, then the Hurricanes and then the Brewsters, flying in a string."

Tired Allison engines came to life and lifted nine of the P-40Es from the runway at 5:30 the morning of March 1, in company with the mixed bag of Hurricanes and Brewsters. Roaring out of the morning sun, the Allied fighters entered a hail of Japanese antiaircraft fire directed from shore batteries as well as a line of about 30 transport

A line of skulls stretches into the distance as the 80th Fighter Group has its collective picture taken, circa 1944–45. Part of 10th Air Force, the 80th FG flew out of India and challenged Japanese operations in Burma. *Air Force photo*

ships anchored parallel to the shore. As barges shuttled troops and materiel from the transports to the beach head, the P-40s, Hurricanes, and Brewsters strafed among the numerous targets. Three of the P-40Es were quickly downed by groundfire. One pilot parachuted perilously near the Japanese lines, but made it back to safety. The sinking of barges was claimed by the Allied force, and a 17th Squadron member wrote, "The line of barges was strung seven or eight deep in columns, so excellent targets were afforded."[133]

The six surviving P-40Es of the 17th Pursuit Squadron (Provisional) returned to Blimbing by 7:40 that morning. All of the Warhawks remaining in the squadron had varying degrees of damage, and no more than a half dozen could have been mustered for any further missions. At 9:00 that morning, a pair of Japanese fighters appeared overhead, and began strafing at will, burning or damaging all of the P-40s. The fall of Java was all but complete; the ranking American officer instructed the men of the 17th to turn in any equipment for use by the Dutch, and to proceed to Jogjakarta. At the end of a wearying day that capped a valiant, but losing, effort over Java, the survivors of the 17th Pursuit Squadron (Provisional) were airlifted by B-17Es on a six-hour flight to the relative safety of Broome, Australia.

Nine P-40 pilots were killed or missing, but all of the aircraft, including supplements, were either destroyed in combat or intentionally demolished to prevent their capture. The squadron claimed 25 Japanese fighters and bombers shot down; confirmation by other sources raised this to 50 aircraft, and the seemingly generous ADC at Soerabaja said the squadron had shot down more than 65 enemy planes! Upon returning to Australia, the 17th Pursuit Squadron (Provisional) was disbanded, its survivors reassigned to various units, and no doubt contributed to the collective wisdom of those gaining squadrons.

Fifty-nine new P-40Es destined to reinforce Java never saw combat. Thirty-two went down at sea aboard the U.S.S. *Langley,* attempting to reach Java but sunk by Japanese bombers on February 27; the remainder, in crates, reached their destination too late to be of use.

P-40Es in the Hands of the Japanese

With a cheerful candor, a Japanese pilot wrote in a Japanese aviation magazine in the 1950s about two airworthy P-40Es captured on Mindanao in the first half of 1942. The article, translated and subsequently published by the American Aviation Historical Society, says two American pilots and their maintenance crews were trapped on Mindanao, and subsequently cooperated with the Japanese, even flying the P-40s to larger airfields to facilitate Japanese recovery of this important intelligence booty. One of the Americans, the article avers, provided the Japanese with details of P-40 performance and tactics, and even flew demonstration sorties on behalf of a Japanese Army Cooperation unit.

When the translated article was published, the positive identity of Americans referred to in the story was unknown. Historians looking at the article have indicated some factual errors were made (even the author excused himself in this regard, acknowledging that his records of those days were subsequently destroyed in B-29 raids on Tokyo). The episode remains enigmatic.[134]

Chinese Allies

The China Air Task Force (CATF) promoted the idea of operations flown by Nationalist Chinese pilots in American warplanes for reasons of manpower and morale. By mid-1943, an Operational Training Unit (OTU) was established in Karachi to hone partially trained Chinese fliers for combat. Old P-40s and B-25s were available for training initially, and were subsequently augmented by more used Warhawks out of North Africa.[135] If Americans had strong sympathies and pro-Chinese sentiment during the war years, the acceptance of Chinese fliers by American airmen was not as universal. One 14th Air Force B-25 pilot who flew combat in 1943 and 1944 bluntly related an experience with Chinese P-40 escorts: "We had an escort of 12 P-40s with Chinese pilots who were flying top cover; we warned them of impending attack by five zeros, and they immediately took cover underneath our bomber formation." To characterize all Chinese pilots with this observation would be a disservice to them. But the melding of Chinese and American combat pilots was not always smooth.

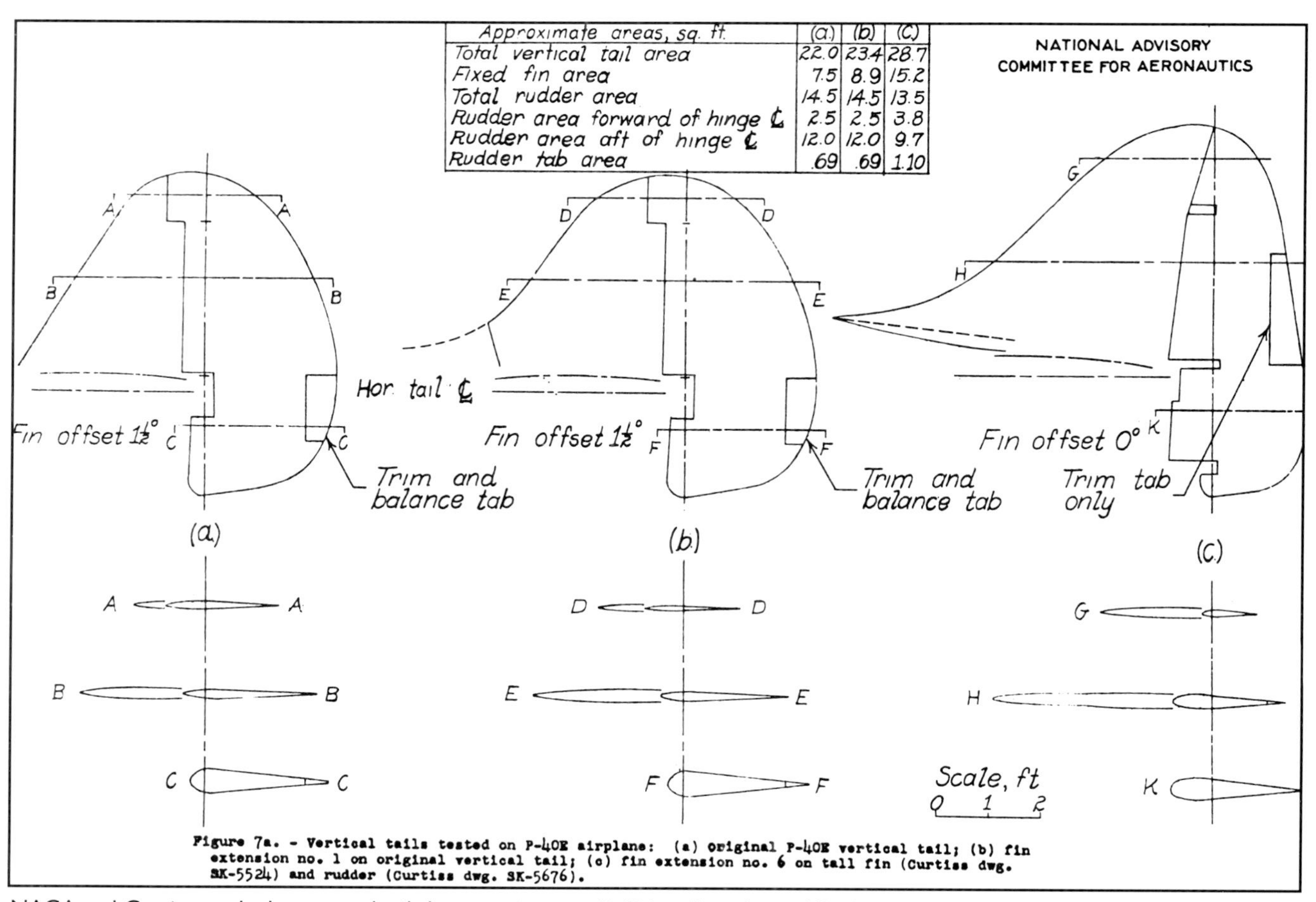

Approximate areas, sq. ft.	(a)	(b)	(c)
Total vertical tail area	22.0	23.4	28.7
Fixed fin area	7.5	8.9	15.2
Total rudder area	14.5	14.5	13.5
Rudder area forward of hinge ℄	2.5	2.5	3.8
Rudder area aft of hinge ℄	12.0	12.0	9.7
Rudder tab area	.69	.69	1.10

Figure 7a. - Vertical tails tested on P-40E airplane: (a) original P-40E vertical tail; (b) fin extension no. 1 on original vertical tail; (c) fin extension no. 6 on tall fin (Curtiss dwg. SK-5524) and rudder (Curtiss dwg. SK-5676).

NACA and Curtiss worked on several tail shapes to improve P-40 handling; the middle design using a broader vertical fin was applied to P-40Ks.

In 1944, the 14th Air Force made a comparison of the "effectiveness of the Chinese air force (P-40s) and selected 14th AF fighter units of comparable strength." Using daily operations and intelligence reports, the 24th Statistical Control Unit made the comparison based on "damage inflicted on the enemy per aircraft in commission and per aircraft on hand, plus a comparison of the maintenance factor, sorties, and sortie rates."[136]

The AAF statisticians relied on the accuracy of reports submitted by the respective AAF and CAF (Chinese Air Force) units. The statistics showed greater effectiveness achieved by the AAF P-40 fliers, although in evaluating the kinds of targets destroyed or damaged during the reporting period, the 24th Statistical Control Unit felt compelled to note, "The data represented . . . (in several of the tables) must be evaluated in the light of the respective missions of the CAF and the forward units of the 14th AF." Chinese P-40s at Chinkiang were mainly detailed to fly close air support of troops at Hengyang. "The Chinese P-40s were thus deprived of the opportunity to destroy massed troops, both infantry and cavalry, on the march, and had few opportunities to hit boats, trains, and other targets which were available to 23rd Group pilots." With that caveat ringing loudly, the statistics showed the AAF flew 6,622 sorties in that time period while CAF P-40s flew 1,394, giving the AAF a sortie rate of 74 per aircraft on hand, and the CAF a rate of 13.9 per aircraft on hand. Once again, an important caveat was emphasized by the statisticians, in an attempt to keep the playing field level, "It is important to keep the supply factor in mind. CAF

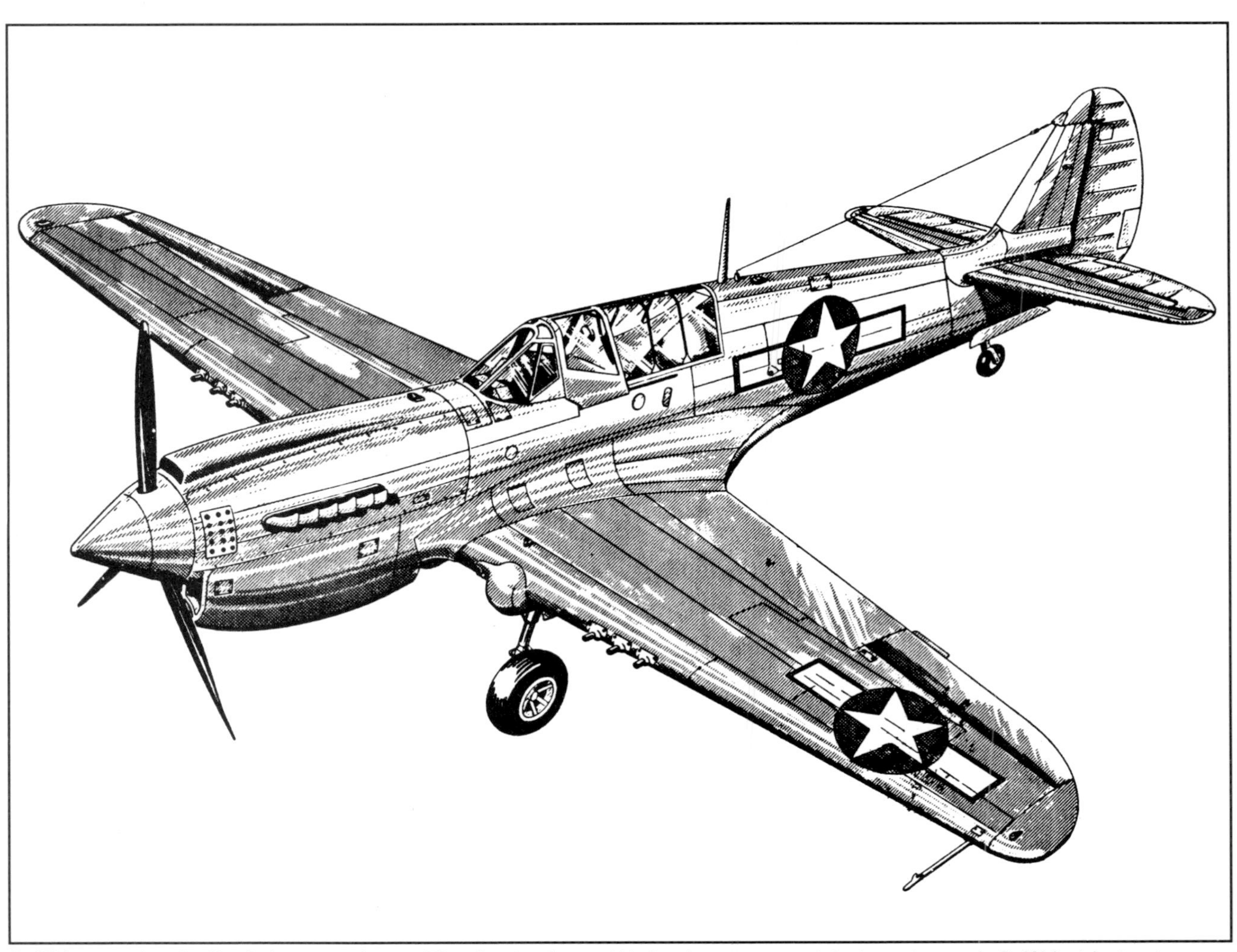

P-40Ns served in the Pacific late into the war. This drawing from a Warhawk parts manual depicts a late-style P-40N with six wing guns. *Wayne Fiamengo collection*

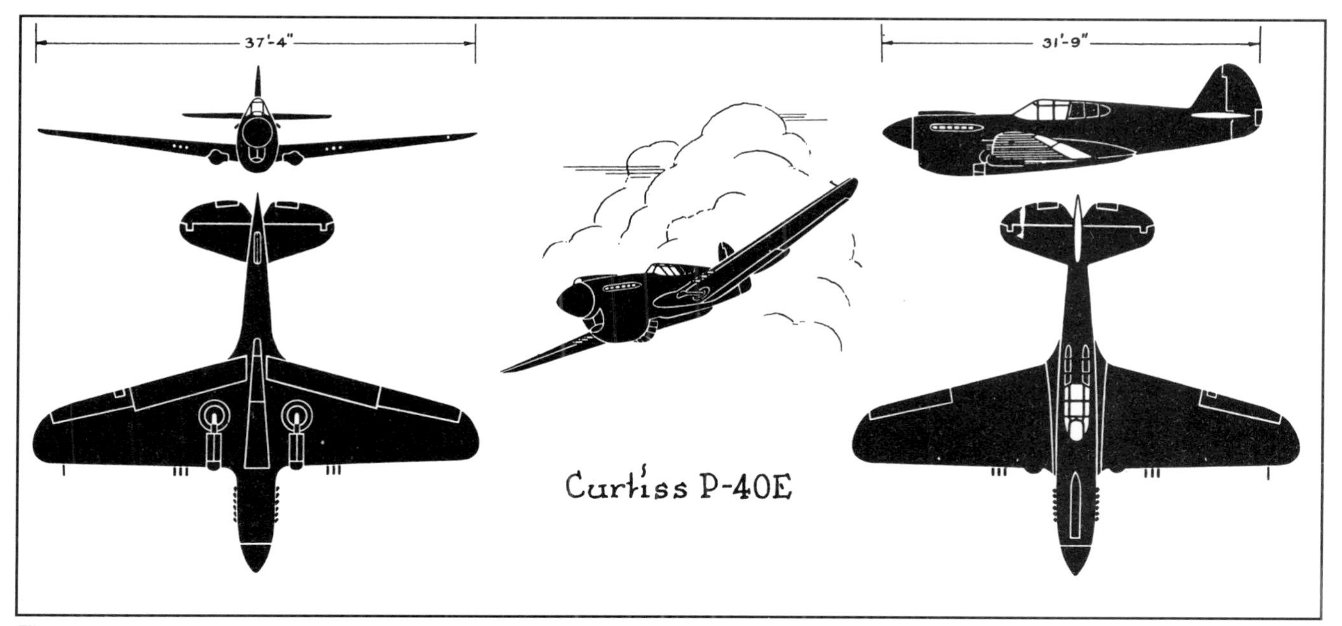

This wartime recognition manual included silhouettes of a P-40E from several angles. *McChord Air Museum collection*

planes were often grounded because of the deficiency in supplies."[137]

If AAF fighters destroyed more targets of every kind tallied, the close-air support role of many of the CAF P-40s showed in a statistic on gun emplacements destroyed, where, with substantially fewer total sorties, CAF P-40s destroyed 45 gun emplacements to the AAF's 59.[138]

If the comparison of AAF and CAF P-40 statistics seems flawed by the caveats duly noted in the report, the episode points out items worthy of note: Some in the 14th AF had misgivings about the contributions of their Chinese counterparts; Chinese fliers were, nonetheless, risking their lives flying combat sorties in American-made Warhawks against the Japanese.

In their landmark books, *The Army Air Forces in World War II,* editors W. F. Craven and J. L. Cate describe a Chinese Air Force operation in which the American-trained and supervised Chinese fliers were considered to be the equal of the current iteration of Japanese pilots in the region.[139]

Snake-Dancing Warhawks over China

In China by 1944, one Warhawk squadron had devised a serpentine flight path that enabled P-40s flying in trail to strafe lightly defended Japanese convoys while keeping an eye peeled for fighter interception. The P-40 pilots spaced their mounts so that every other Warhawk in the serpent dance was firing on a portion of the convoy as the nonfiring elements of the flight were rounding out their S-turns, to get back in firing position just as the first set of strafers began their own S-turns. The effect was to suppress small arms fire while hosing each truck of a convoy. An AAF intelligence summary explained, "The attack gave each plane a chance to strafe the entire length of the column and effectively prevented the enemy from organizing concentrated ground fire." The S-turns afforded a wide degree of visibility, enabling the P-40 pilots to scan for Japanese fighters. "On the first mission using these tactics," the AAF summary noted, "four P-40s destroyed 23 trucks and 6 horses along the road from Loyang to Loning. Only two holes were found in the planes on their return."[140]

Requiem for the Warhawk

Compelling reasons may have existed to argue for replacing the P-40 in combat by 1944. As early as March 1943, a Curtiss representative was urging his company to ensure long-range capabilities for the P-40, to keep it competitive in the leapfrog long-distance Pacific war. In some cases, it may have been as fundamental as logistics; if fewer, and newer, fighter types could be fielded, supplying and maintaining them would become easier. But

Early camouflaged P-40s like this example gave American fighter pilots some flying experience—though sometimes not enough—in the type before combat was thrust upon them in December 1941. *Bowers collection*

the P-40 did not leave without a salute from its friends—the men who had relied on it in combat.

When the 49th Fighter Group of the Fifth Air Force swapped its Warhawks for Lightnings in September 1944, it was not without fanfare. The Group history for that month noted: "A peek through the dust at the airstrip would reveal the Seventh and Eighth Squadron pilots bidding farewell to their faithful P-40s and undergoing a rigorous training program to acquaint themselves with the twin-engined P-38. Although many pilots were reluctant to make the change because of a fond nostalgic feeling for the Kittyhawks and Warhawks, they realized the advantages of the increased range and speed gained with the P-38. Let no man be foolish enough to make any slightly disparaging remark about a P-40 to these pilots, else the foolhardy one find himself pinned down by an extremely irate fighter pilot whose respect for that plane will never dwindle. As an all 'round rugged fighter and dive-bomber the '40 will never be forgotten by the old 49ers who flew them from Darwin to Biak, fighting, bombing, and strafing."[141]

British Pioneers and American Allies in North Africa

RAF's Air Marshal Coningham Excelled with Desert Hawks

The acknowledged architect of modern tactical air operations, British Air Marshal Sir Arthur Coningham went on assignment to the Middle East in July 1941, where he soon embraced Curtiss Tomahawks and later Kittyhawks, judiciously applying them to support Army units in combat, while shunning the notion of having standing elements of airpower parceled out to protect the Army regardless of specific situations. Coningham, a tall New Zealander self-described as an athlete, not a student, was, nonetheless, the professor when it came to tactical

By mid-1941, the RAF was employing Tomahawk IIAs and Bs (similar to this Curtiss model H81-A-2 Tomahawk IIA, number AH973) in North Africa. This Curtiss factory photo shows a quirk of assembly, in which the fuselage roundel was applied before the large wing fillet was screwed in place, with the fillet subsequently blocking part of the yellow ring surrounding the roundel. *Curtiss Wright photo via Peter M. Bowers*

The first Kittyhawk I, with revised nose contours, comparable to the P-40D, gave the British a P-40 with improved performance in the North African desert. *Curtiss Wright via Peter M. Bowers*

airpower in North Africa. By the fall of 1941, Coningham took some comfort in having large enough numbers of Tomahawks and Hurricanes to somewhat make up for their performance shortcomings versus the latest Messerschmitt 109 variants arriving in the theater. At the same time, he exercised some restraint in levying requests for Spitfires to counter the German fighter menace, lest stridence should cost him favor within the RAF back home.[142]

Coningham's North African war had its origins in Benito Mussolini's erring attempts there beginning 10 June 1940. The British quickly countered and took Italy's colonies at Eritrea, Somaliland, and Ethiopia. By early 1941, the determined British forces were poised to take Libya from Italian control. In February of that year, the German Army committed two divisions to North Africa in an effort to save the territorial holdings of its Axis partner. For the next year and a half, the British were confronted with a new, capable foe in General Erwin Rommel's *Afrika Korps*. For a time, it appeared even Egypt would fall to the advancing Germans. The British Eighth Army prevailed, but Rommel was far from defeated.[143]

Viewing this scenario, Allied planners labored over the need to open another front against Germany, specifically to take some pressure off the beleaguered Soviet Union. A meaningful Allied invasion of Europe could not be mounted in 1942, and North Africa became the focus for an American/British invasion to augment British forces already there. Such an invasion, if successful and sustainable, promised two good outcomes for the Allies: The neutralizing of Axis strength in that region, and the diversion of German assets away from the Russian front.

By March of 1942, still more than a half year away from the Allied invasion, Coningham's aerial resources included newly arrived P-40D variants, which the RAF christened Kittyhawk I. Distinguishable from the earlier Tomahawk by its revised nose contour, owing to the shape of its new-model Allison engine with spur reduction gear, more than 500 of the Kittyhawk Is were taken on by the RAF. As Middle Eastern RAF units debugged their new Kittyhawk Is in the spring of 1942, Coningham still could not count on a fighter with speed enough to intercept the newest Me-109s, but he had a factory-made bomb hauler, as the P-40D was designed with a centerline shackle for up to a 500-pound bomb as well as positions for smaller bombs under the wings.

Coningham would need his Kittyhawks and Tomahawks to execute aspects of his tactical air philosophy when German General Rommel launched a well-supplied attack in late May 1942 that forced a British retreat and the loss of most of the British garrison with embattled Tobruk. Coningham employed continual fighter sweeps over the battlefield when Rommel's offensive at the battle of Gazala began May 26. Early on, Coningham ordered his fighter forces to limit their altitude to 6,000 feet and concentrate on ground attacks against German lines of supply. Coningham was praised for his use of fighter-bombers, but the lack of replacement aircraft in large quantities prompted a return to more traditional fighter roles. Coningham now predicted a race among the combatants to field large numbers of fighter-bombers. Locally modified variants of the Curtiss Kittyhawks, dubbed "Kittybombers," could now lug a pair of 250-pound bombs and subsequently defend themselves fairly well against Luftwaffe fighters. American bomb racks made the Kittybomber possible, and Coningham wanted to so equip all of his Kittyhawk squadrons.[144]

On June 17, as the British were evacuating their endangered garrison from El Adem as Rommel pressed onward, Coningham's reconnaissance told him of a forward Luftwaffe airfield, too new to have antiaircraft defenses yet installed. Gambling, the Germans had moved fighters to the new field in order to hunt among the retreating British forces. But Sir Arthur Coningham's Kittyhawks arrived overhead to find the Luftwaffe fighters refueling and rearming. With no antiaircraft defenses, the enemy airplanes were decimated by the Curtiss fighters, thereby purchasing an orderly withdrawal for the British Army troops.[145]

Rommel's efforts to take Cairo stumbled on 21 June 1942, when his invasion of Egypt was thwarted by determined British ground units enjoying air superiority in that area. When his warplanes went on the offensive, Coningham sometimes sent bombers escorted by bomb-laden Kittybombers close in on either side, while clean-configured Kittyhawks (or sometimes Spitfires) flew top cover. Ideally, the approach of the bomber force toward an infantry-escorted tank column would send Axis troops tumbling from

Creating their own sandstorm, RAF 250 Squadron Kittyhawk IIIs—P-40K variants—taxi on the unpaved North African desert. Machine gun shell ejection ports under the wing appear to be taped over, possibly as a sand baffle. Gun muzzles on fighters often were taped, with the first airborne firing of the guns popping open the protective tape.

their vehicles, thereby diminishing any light antiaircraft response they could mount. This afforded the Kittybombers relative safety for low-level attacks.[146] As early as July 1942, numbers of American P-40s would be added to the aerial mixture over North Africa, some arriving by U.S. Navy aircraft carriers that November during Operation Torch. The P-40 would be an integral part of the Allied Mediterranean air armada, from 1941 in North Africa on up into attacks on Italy in 1944.

American Interest

The global battlefield of 1941, even before American entry into the hostilities, was a school of experience, a constantly changing classroom in which U.S. Army Air Corps observers made reports back home. Lieutenant W. W. Momyer departed Washington, D.C., on 23 March 1941 on such a fact-finding tour, arriving in Cairo exactly a month later. Traveling around the Middle East, Lieutenant Momyer's assignment involved maintenance on RAF P-40B equivalents.[147] What he learned about the British experience in maintaining P-40s in the desert environment could ease American efforts to do the same, should that become necessary.

Lieutenant Momyer found the British working on their Tomahawks in a vacuum of information; many manuals had not arrived with the American fighters, he said. "When I arrived, there were no technical orders or written instructions on American equipment in the entire Middle East Command. There were very few British mechanics who had ever seen American equipment." This caused a variety of mishaps of varying severity. Momyer related: "A number of canopies were flying off in flight which had caused a good deal of concern by the British. I checked a reported failure, and found that the mechanics were failing to safety the canopy catch and also not putting the rear part of the canopy on the canopy track. . . . The technical orders covering the canopy arrived three months after they had the airplanes." Momyer showed his British hosts how to do these things and virtually eliminated canopy departures.[148]

En route to North Africa, the U.S. Navy held target practice at sea while men tended P-40s being carried to the war front aboard the *U.S.S. Ranger* in November 1942.

Hell's Belles, parked in North Africa circa 1943, shows its Merlin-engine multipurpose chin scoop to advantage. Light-duty wing bomb shackles and heavier centerline braces are visible. *Air Force*

The Air Corps lieutenant was unequivocal in his description of his natural surroundings: "Maintaining an airplane on the Western Desert (of North Africa) was the most severe test an airplane could undergo. The camp was spread over a seven mile area. Airplanes, when subjected to bombing and ground strafing, must be dispersed at least with 400 yards between airplanes. The airplanes were covered when not in flight and during the night, but even then could not keep the sand out. When a sandstorm blows it is difficult to see 50 yards on the field."

Lieutenant Momyer expressed surprise when British mechanics "made no effort to throw up a protection around the airplane when working in the sand. They allowed sand to get in anything they uncovered." But the stout P-40 survived quite well under these primitive conditions. "Even maintaining the airplane as inefficient(ly) as this it seemed to keep going with a minimum amount of trouble," he added. The British Tomahawk mechanics faced a dilemma with lubricated parts trapping sand which acted like an abrasive. "It may be necessary to sacrifice good lubrication in preference to allowing sand to wear away any moving part. Some control cables were found with only a few strands of wire remaining. Also controls were often found jammed due to sand collecting around pulleys," Momyer recorded.

The Curtiss Electric propellers of the early Tomahawks in the desert would get stuck in low-pitch, high-rpm, settings because a relief valve would not seat properly when sand entered it. The problem could be rectified by cleaning, but this sometimes meant the loss of a vital P-40 for two or three hours. Sparkplugs also fouled earlier in the desert than in stateside operations.

Operations from sand strips included a healthy dose of groundloops as the British fliers got accustomed to the P-40s' landing gear quirks. "Of all the crack-ups," Lieutenant Momyer said, "90 percent were from ground loops. One squadron, over a period of two months, cracked up 28 airplanes landing, and lost only three in combat." Momyer observed some of the British pilots made hard landings on the main gear rather than three-point touchdowns. Crosswind landings in the RAF P-40s were made, with the Curtiss landing gear vulnerable to shearing from the side load. The American lieutenant noted, "The (Hawker) Hurricane had

The Tennessean, a Merlin Warhawk of the 79th Fighter Group in North Africa, also carried the 85th Fighter Squadron's flying skull decoration. Casual garb belied serious warriors who acquitted themselves, and their Warhawks, in North Africa. *Air Force*

cross bracing on the landing gear that will take a sidewise landing; the P-40 is not built for that type of stress and will not take it."[149]

The RAF's main facility for assembling arriving P-40s was a leftover base from World War I at Abu Suweir, about 10 miles from the banks of the Suez Canal. When Lieutenant Momyer visited in 1941, Abu Suweir was the main port for overhauling and supplying aircraft for use in the Western Desert. Momyer was not impressed with what he found there. "The personnel as a whole were untrained mechanics, and had no opportunity to attend a mechanics' school. Tools were obsolete and wholly inadequate. It was taking five to six days to turn a P-40 out ready for combat," he stated. In the lieutenant's view, this inefficiency explained why there were only three P-40 squadrons operating in the desert at that time (one of which, the 112 Squadron, is credited with originating the sharkmouth that ultimately became indelibly linked with the Flying Tigers). "The production at this base wasn't sufficient to keep the existing squadrons re-equipped, let alone outfit new squadrons," Momyer said. When American civilian personnel arrived, production quickened to two P-40s a day.

Lacking sufficient numbers of mechanics at Abu Suweir, the British were forced to combine the preferably distinct tasks of assembly and overhaul, sometimes taking mechanics away from assembling newly arrived P-40s to have them overhaul worn Curtisses. Inspections that Lieutenant Momyer estimated should require six hours "took two to three days, which I thought was an excessive amount of time when the airplanes were needed so badly on the Western Desert."

British P-40 operations in 1941, when Lieutenant Momyer visited, consisted of multiple tiers. Advanced landing fields at Sidi Barani, just sufficient to fuel and arm the fighters, were not geared for heavy maintenance. The Curtisses did not remain there overnight because of the hazards of nocturnal Axis bombers. "The next field behind this was the operational landing ground which was about 100 miles further back. Here the squadron was stationed," Momyer wrote. Another 200 miles to the rear, the base landing ground handled periodic inspections and modifications to the British P-40s. A chronic shortage of P-40 spare parts at this time caused a high rate of grounding.

A bright spot in the sometimes bleak picture

of early British P-40 combat in the desert was the durability of the Allison engine. Where Momyer noted Hurricanes with Rolls Merlin engines being changed after only 65 to 95 hours of operation, usually for compression loss, one of the P-40s "had 140 hours of operation time and was still going with good compression. This P-40 was operating without an air filter which made it more startling that it was still in operation. The P-40 up to this time had stood the desert very well and the British were very well satisfied with its performance. On the whole I think the P-40 stood up exceptionally well. . . ." Other RAF users of American aircraft would later compound the tales of rugged Allison engines continuing to function under circumstances that might have taxed the superb, if perhaps finicky, Merlin.

Lieutenant Momyer concluded his observations of P-40B operations in the Western Desert with several succinct suggestions borne of the hardships he experienced while in Egypt. He urged "that all guns for desert operations in pursuit airplanes be housed in the wing completely." (The P-40B equivalents still had cowling guns; possibly the invasion of sand into the engine compartment when servicing guns prompted the remark.) Momyer also said all civilian technicians considered for duty in the region "be given a physical examination and those having gastric trouble, sinus trouble, lung and chest trouble, not be allowed to go to Egypt."[150] It was due to trips like the lieutenant's that operations and maintenance of P-40s overseas improved. If he occasionally found fault with British ways of dealing with their early P-40s, the problems were curable, and the will of the RAF to prosecute the war was manifest as they mounted their Tomahawks day in, day out in the grinding war against Rommel.

Lieutenant Momyer's star continued to rise in the AAF; in June 1942, as a major, he became commander of the P-40-equipped 33rd Fighter Group.

When the Watkins brothers, flying P-40s in the 325th and 79th Fighter Groups, met in North Africa at L. G. Har North in May 1943, a photographer capturing the scene included portions of a P-40 showing the placement of the American flag on the lower surface of the left wing, as seen on a number of P-40s in North Africa. Unsure of initial French reaction to a mixed British/American invasion there, effort was made to emphasize the American component of the force. *Air Force*

Warhawks Carry the Torch

Political sensitivities suggested the American/British invasion of North Africa—Operation Torch—set for November 1942 should appear as much as possible to be an American event. With France occupied by Germany, Vichy French forces in the region would be less likely to resist American entry than they would British additions, planners believed. Many of the P-40s dispatched to the Mediterranean aboard U.S. Navy aircraft carriers were emblazoned with prominent American flags painted on their fuselages and wings. It was as if the trademark of democracy were being used as a talisman in the face of an uncertain reception.

In serving up a flotilla for Torch, the U.S. Navy earmarked for its own aircraft the aircraft carriers *Ranger, Santee, Sangamon,* and *Charger*, the latter three being auxiliaries. Initially the Navy balked at turning the *Charger* over to ferrying AAF fighters for Torch, even though P-40Es had been test-catapulted successfully at the Navy's own facility in Philadelphia (and, in a real-world precursor, P-40E pilots of the 73rd Fighter Squadron launched from the U.S.S. *Saratoga* to bolster the garrison at Midway in mid-June 1942). Naval planners expressed concerns over whether or not the intended Merlin-powered P-40Fs could take the strain of catapulting. They further argued that to use land-based aircraft in the initial assault was tantamount to sacrificing the Warhawks because they would have no place to land until an airfield could be secured. Ultimately, another carrier, the U.S.S. *Chenango,* was chosen to carry the 77 P-40s of the 33rd Fighter Group. Following the *Chenango* in another convoy bound for Casablanca, the British auxiliary carrier *Archer* packed another 35 replacement P-40s.[151]

The Allied occupation of the Port Lyautey Airfield signaled time for the 33rd Group's P-40Fs to launch from the *Chenango,* which they began doing on 10 November 1942. An AAF study noted, "However, Navy shells and dive-bombers had badly damaged the main runway at Port Lyautey and the rest of the field was soft." The catapulting had to be suspended, but was finished over the next two days. The AAF study reported,

The high value of ground attack aircraft in North Africa led to modifications like this dual belly mount on a 79th Fighter Group P-40, carrying a pair of British bombs. This lash-up saw some use in Tunisia. *Air Force*

This flag-emblazoned AAF long-body P-40F of the 33rd Fighter Group in North Africa (circa mid-December 1942) showed British-style camouflage, and yellow rings around star insignia. Prominent American flags adorned many P-40s in the early stages of North African AAF fighting. *Marty Isham collection*

"Of the 77 P-40s launched from the *Chenango,* one crashed into the sea, another was never heard from, and 17 were damaged in landing. The 33rd Group took no part in the remainder of the action against the French, terminated on 11 November by armistice negotiations."[152] This outcome partially vindicated naysayers in the Navy, as well as some in the AAF, who said the Casablanca region could be overwhelmed with too many land-based aircraft initially, and who suggested sending the Warhawks to Egypt to help secure air superiority there instead. However, the immediate presence ashore of the 33rd Fighter Group's Merlin-powered P-40s permitted the Navy aircraft carriers and planes to depart by 13 November.

When the *Archer* arrived offshore not long after, the 35 attrition-replacement P-40s led by Maj. Phillip Cochran catapulted for the flight to Port Lyautey, where 4 cracked up on landing. Major Cochran was to become a legend in the Mediterranean; a keen exploiter of the P-40's abilities.

P-40s Against Axis Fighters in the Middle East

Nearly two years after American Lt. W. W. Momyer observed British P-40 operations in the Western Desert, a Curtiss representative noted relative air-to-air strengths and weaknesses of P-40s in that region in February 1943, after USAAF units added to the number of the Curtiss fighters operating there. By that time, the P-40F and K models had been pitted against the Me-109F and G variants, the FW-190, and the Italian Macchi 202 fighter, as well as friendly comparisons with Spitfire Vs and Hurricanes. The Curtiss representative noted: "Top speed was satisfactory until just recently when the higher speed enemy fighters have been contacted with true speeds ranging . . . to 390 miles per hour. In order to have a fighter cope with (the) 109G, Macchi 202, (and) Focke-Wulf 190, the airplane must be able to climb to 20,000 (feet) at the rate of at least 3,000 feet per minute. In the type of air warfare in this area, this

This AAF short-body P-40F in North Africa shows an unorthodox serial number painted on rudder fabric, with RAF-style fin flash ahead of that. Prominent in the cockpit is the gunsight, potentially a source of injury in crash landings if the pilot's shoulder harness did not keep him restrained far enough back in the seat. *Howard Levy via Peter M. Bowers*

one fact has always left the P-40 on the defensive." Enemy fighters enjoyed the ability to climb to safety, out of reach of the P-40. Conversely, and fortunately for the P-40 pilots, the Curtiss representative noted, "one of the exceedingly valuable characteristics of the P-40 is its unusual high diving speeds and its acceleration in a dive. This one feature has been responsible for some of its many successes."[153]

The P-40 had a tight turning radius that served it well, the Curtiss employee related. "If they (P-40 pilots in the Middle East) keep their formations and turn into an enemy attacking from behind, the attacking plane usually overshoots," because the Axis fighters typically started their attacks from above, and in a high-speed descent could not turn with the P-40s. If a P-40 and a Macchi 202 were at the same speed, the Italian fighter could turn with the P-40. With a top speed around 370 miles per hour and a swift rate of climb, the Macchi 202 "is a very difficult airplane for the P-40 to meet."

The Curtiss representative opined that in combat against a P-40, the Macchi 202s "are considered more dangerous than the 109s due to the fact that they have about the same performance as the 109, yet possess a turning radius about the same as the P-40F."[154]

The fortunes of war held deadly surprises; in a classic formation turning maneuver to thwart a lone Me-109G over the Tunisian coast on 30 April 1943, a P-40 flight leader collided with another flight leader in the turn. Often, midairs are not clean; a bloom of dust and bits of aircraft dirty the sky and then it's over except for the rain of wreckage. After the mission, P-40F pilot Capt. Barney Turner of the 86th Fighter Squadron laconically reported the scene: "I pulled up to avoid the crash. My wingman slid under the two to avoid the crash and both planes fell on him. The ME (Me-109) had pulled up and came right in front of me and seemed to hang there at 6,000 or 7,000 feet. I fired one very long burst. He rolled over on his back and fell straight down into the water. . . . Confirmed by Lieutenant Brewer." Only a momentary geyser of sea foam marked the watery grave of the Messerschmitt. The fog of battle, in alliance with the elements of chance and skill, had played out a deadly vignette that would be erased and staged anew time and again over the next two years.[155]

Those Who Served

As World War II began, the Warhawk symbolized USAAF fighters and the hopeful arsenal of democracy. Rugged, single-place, and bearing aloft a pilot with the will to win, the P-40 was home to many fliers, and the responsibility of resourceful builders and maintainers. Some of those who served with P-40s and animated them gave a legacy of courage.

Pilot John R. Alison, 8th Pursuit Group and 23rd Fighter Group

"When those bullets hit the armor plate, they make a lot of noise." Retired Major General John R. Alison recalled a predicament in which he rode a rudderless P-40 while a Japanese fighter pilot poured fire into Alison's Warhawk in an effort to down the Curtiss fighter. In what was to be his next-to-last P-40 mission, Alison, at the request of Gen. Claire Chennault, had gone up to Liang Shan, China, to fly with some new Chinese P-40 pilots in the summer of 1943. Part of a flight of two American-manned and seven Nationalist Chinese Warhawks assigned to escort nine B-24 Liberators, Alison was about to reconnoiter an opening in an undercast for the bombers when black specks materialized out of the clouds like a dash of pepper thrown in the air. The specks were many Japanese fighters, and the contingent of P-40s met the challenge. Alison watched one enemy fighter plunge into a cloud bank before his guns, a probable victim; a second, confirmed victory, exploded, and then he pulled up into a near-stall, depressing the trigger switch in an effort to distract three Japanese fighters above him as they dived toward the B-24s.

Alison's Warhawk was in this perilous climb when a Japanese fighter raced up from beneath and managed to put a bullet squarely on the P-40's rudder hinge. The rounded Curtiss rudder was ripped from the plane, leaving Alison with a marginally flyable P-40 that had no hope of engaging in combat maneuvering. Alison got on the radio. "If somebody doesn't help me, I'm gone," he recalled later. The other American flier in the Warhawk flight could not find Alison's crippled P-40 in the wildly zooming melee. The Japanese fighter pilot kept hammering Alison's Warhawk from behind. "He hit me, and hit me, and hit me," Alison remembered. One round lodged in the armor plate behind his seat as others clanked against it. "He was shooting through my rear gas tank." Soon Alison saw the air around him come alive with gunfire. One of the Chinese P-40 pilots was on the tail of the preoccupied Japanese fighter, pouring fire from his .50-caliber machine guns into the enemy plane, with the concentrated firepower of the Chinese Warhawk also whipping past Alison's rudderless fighter. "I thought he was going to get us both," Alison said of the Chinese pilot. But only the Japanese plane fell in the onslaught from the Nationalist Chinese P-40's guns, allowing Alison to escape and nurse his riddled Warhawk back to the grass strip at Liang Shan. World War I ace Eddie Rickenbacker, who was on hand to fly with Alison out of the theater as John's tour was over, watched as Alison lowered his P-40's landing gear only to expose two useless main tires, shot up in the running fight. The P-40 dug into the turf and stood upon its nose; though not the sort of landing Alison wanted to make in front of Rickenbacker, the harrowing event and its outcome did credit both to the plane and its pilot.[156]

Alison saw his first P-40 in 1940 when he was a pilot in the Eighth Pursuit Group at Langley Field, Virginia. Already flying Curtiss P-36s, which used essentially the same airframe behind a stubby radial engine, the men of the Eighth Group quickly checked out in long-nosed P-40s as a qualified pilot stood on the wing and pointed out operational features before turning the fliers loose for their first P-40 takeoff. Alison liked the handling traits of the older P-36, and at first he felt the P-40 was less maneuverable until he got the hang of the long-nosed newcomer. As prewar P-40 mishap photos attest, the longer nose of the P-40 prompted a rash of nose-overs and groundloops until pilots learned not to over-apply brakes during landing; Alison managed to avoid that predicament, he said. Another landing problem with P-40s soon manifested itself, "When you came in to land, you had a stall characteristic with that long nose high in front," Alison explained. "It could get away and ground loop."

Alison mastered the P-40, and together with Hubert "Hub" Zemke, he went to the Soviet Union in mid-1941 to test Tomahawks assembled by the Soviets and a cadre of about five British mechanics, using aircraft originally intended for Britain that were shipped by sea. "Hub and I test flew each of the airplanes and turned them over to the Russians." The assembly base was a marvel of civil engineering in the marshy land near Archangel. A 5,000-foot runway and taxiways were made firm by planking six-inch-by-six-inch timbers on top of two layers of felled trees, Alison said. Conversation with Soviet pilots was handled by Russian interpreters; Alison and Zemke were not permitted to visit a forward Soviet operational base where the Tomahawks were employed. After testing each fighter, the Americans could only turn them over to the Soviets, with whom there was little fraternization.[157]

P-40s, including this B-model, carried gasoline in a large tank behind the pilot's seat. *Bowers collection*

Alison's duties as assistant military air attaché to the Soviet Union could be frustrating, and he clamored for a combat assignment as the United States entered the war. First dispatched to the Middle East where he worked in Iraq and Iran, a wire from Gen. Hap Arnold ordered Alison to China in mid-1942. "I arrived at Kunming in the middle of June 1942," Alison recalled. General Chennault's fabled Flying Tigers, the American Volunteer Group, were about to stand down, their task being taken up by the USAAF's 23rd Fighter Group, part of the China Air Task Force (CATF). Only a few of the original Tigers stayed on, and Alison was assigned to be deputy to 75th Fighter Squadron commander Tex Hill, a veteran of the AVG. When Hill departed a few months later, Alison became squadron commander, until moving up to deputy group commander in 1943.

Alison said when he arrived in China in 1942, a spate of groundlooping incidents with P-40s prompted Chennault to request that General Arnold sendonly experienced P-40 pilots to the 23rd Fighter Group. In one 18-day stretch, Alison said, the outfit sustained about 17 groundloops in P-40s. Fortunately, not all resulted in material damage.

Alison's first aerial victories happened during a night interception of Japanese bombers in about August of 1942. In that fight, he downed two bombers and got a probable on another. "And they shot me down," he added. In the inky skies, Alison strained to see the enemy formation he was trying to close with. Exhaust flames, invisible in the light of day, were the nocturnal beacons that enabled Alison to home in on the Japanese bombers and dispatch some of them.

Depth perception and relative speeds were more difficult to judge in the dim light, and Alison tried to slow his P-40 as he overran the Japanese aircraft, and wound up in the middle of their for-

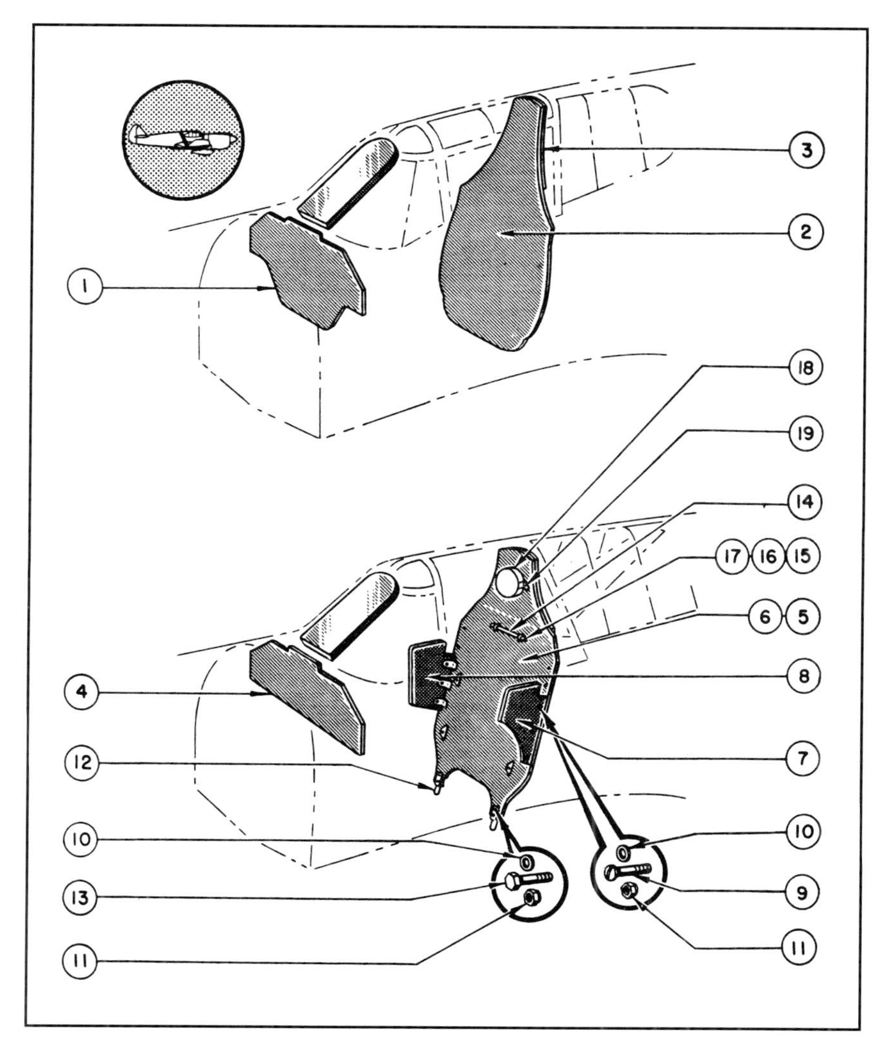

Armor plate behind the pilot's seat saved P-40 pilot John Alison's life in the summer of 1943. Armor variations illustrated in a Warhawk manual included one version with cockpit side protection; the curved cutout on the left side piece probably accommodated engine throttle quadrant. Other P-40s had only rear and frontal protection. *Wayne Fiamengo collection*

mation. Before Alison could open fire, a broadside from a bomber punched a five-inch hole in the rugged V-1710 engine's crankcase. A Japanese bullet had penetrated his parachute. His left arm was blistered, possibly from a Japanese tracer round. On fire with a failing engine, Alison's P-40 kept working long enough for him to destroy three of the Japanese bombers. "That engine kept running," he recalled. But not indefinitely—when it became obvious he could not stretch his flight back to base, Alison plunked the P-40 into a river nearby, quenching the flames in 14 feet of water. The crash-landing held a special peril for Alison, he recalled. That P-40E had been equipped with a British shoulder harness of a design that Alison found too restrictive when he needed to swivel his head in the heat of battle, to keep the enemy in sight. So he did not fasten the harness, and upon impact with the water, "I put my face in the gunsight and I got cut up a bit," he explained.[158]

More than a half century has passed since Alison engaged in life-and-death combat over the skies of China in a P-40, where he logged one ground and six aerial claims over Japanese warplanes. He went on to attain the rank of major general, and served as president and chairman of the Air Force Association. Following his Air Force career with a stint at Northrop Aircraft, Alison met up with the Chinese pilot who saved his life when Northrop sold F-5s to Nationalist China in the 1960s. Looking back, Alison had fond memories of the P-40 series. "They all flew very well," he remembered, although landing a Warhawk was more difficult than landing a P-51 with its wider landing gear track. The P-40K was his favorite of all the models he flew. Would General Alison want to fly a P-40 again if he had the chance? "I'd love to own one."

Remnant from the movie *Tora! Tora! Tora!*, this replica P-40E made of fiberglass and spare parts, including Beech 18 outer wings, stood as a gate guardian at Wheeler Field when photographed 50 years after the attack on Pearl Harbor. *Author photo*

Pilots George "Wheaties" Welch and Kenneth Taylor, USAAF

Wheaties Welch—nicknamed because he quickly generated energy, like the cereal of the same name—was a confident young second lieutenant posted to Wheeler Field in the tropical paradise of the Territory of Hawaii in prewar 1941. He familiarized himself with the lush and dazzling beauty of the islands on flights in P-40s that soon would take on life-and-death urgency.

When Japanese Naval warplanes appeared over Oahu, violating a sleepy Sunday morning, Welch's characteristic quickness vaulted him into action and into the cockpit of a Curtiss P-40 Tomahawk. Overcoming the initial element of surprise enjoyed by the Japanese at Pearl Harbor, Welch etched his name in history that morning by becoming the first fighter to shoot down a Japanese aircraft at Pearl.

As bombs fell and aircraft roared overhead, Welch and Lt. Kenneth Taylor bolted outside where they saw a pall of smoke over Pearl Harbor. Nobody had to tell Welch and Taylor what to do next; with no warning, the two new fighter pilots were thrust into the thick of a world war, at peace one instant and calculating combat moves the next. Taylor called up to maintenance crews at a little grass strip at Haleiwa some 10 miles distant, hopeful that the 47th Pursuit Squadron P-40s sent there for gunnery practice had escaped the fate of those aircraft demolished at Wheeler.

Welch and Taylor barreled along the road to Haleiwa, only sure of what they'd witnessed, and not equipped with any comprehensive information about the attacking Japanese force. Nor did they have authorization to go after the attackers, but that point mattered little to a pair of young fighter pilots watching their tranquil world shattered by other pilots from a foreign land. The Tomahawks Welch and Taylor climbed into at Haleiwa had ammunition only for their small .30-caliber wing machine guns, and not the twin .50-calibers nested in the nose.

Wheaties Welch lined up on a dive-bomber over the Marine Corps airfield at Ewa, emptying enough .30-caliber rounds into the Japanese warplane to send it earthward. Meanwhile, Taylor dispatched another Japanese airplane over Ewa. It was a raw and startling sensation for Welch, shooting and being shot at in earnest. When a gunner in a multiplace Japanese bomber put bullets into Welch's P-40, the young lieutenant masked his aircraft with cloud cover long enough to verify the damage was not mortal before he emerged to re-enter the fray. Welch and Taylor soon each claimed their second victory of the morning in the humid skies as their .30-caliber ammunition supply dwindled.[159]

The two lieutenants landed their dark olive drab P-40s at Wheeler Field to re-arm, throttling up their Tomahawks for takeoff just as a wave of Japanese bombers escorted by fighters set upon Wheeler. Welch succeeded in downing a fighter that had beset Taylor, even as Wheaties' P-40 took more hits. Wheeling over the verdant Oahu terrain in a deadly game of aerial tag, Welch downed what was to be his fourth and final Japanese warplane of the day before settling back at Haleiwa to reload for another go at the enemy. His P-40 continued to perform as Welch lifted off from the grass for a third foray that morning, but the Japanese aircraft had done their worst, and were out to sea, winging back to the aircraft carriers that had brought them within striking distance of American territory.

In recounting events of the day, Welch has been credited with downing the first Japanese plane that day, followed momentarily by Taylor's first kill. Distinguished Service Crosses awaited Lieutenants Welch and Taylor for their quick actions over Pearl Harbor. Wheaties Welch continued his Pacific combat career in P-39s—using the Airacobra to down three more Japanese warplanes—and P-38 Lightnings, in which he ultimately ran his string of victories up to 16.

Welch's credentials in the cockpit led to his hiring as a test pilot for North American Aviation after the war, under whose auspices he made the first flight in the new XP-86 (later F-86) Sabre jet fighter on 1 October 1947.

On 12 October 1954, during a Mach 1.5 dive in a Super Sabre at Edwards Air Force Base, Wheaties Welch met the fate that he had escaped during so many combat hours, when the supersonic jet crashed, killing the fighter pilot known for his energy and his quickness in combat in a P-40 over Pearl Harbor.

Ken Glassburn, 35th Pursuit Group

Ken Glassburn was a newly graduated second lieutenant with silver wings who wanted to fly heavy bombers in California in the summer of 1941. His orders sent him there, but the bombers had shifted to another base, so Lieutenant Glassburn was summarily decreed to be a P-40 fighter pilot at Hamilton Field, north of San Francisco. That is where Glassburn first saw a P-40. The 35th Pursuit Group brought new fliers like Glassburn into the fold gradually, bridging their limited experience in AT-6 Texan trainers with a few hops in a Curtiss P-36A before launching them in the similar P-40.

The radial-engined P-36A taught lessons to young Lieutenant Glassburn in a hurry; with no second seat, he had to master it solo. "The first time I started down the runway," Ken recalled, "I wasn't quite up on the torque on that baby." The P-36 was a handful, compared with the AT-6. Workmen beside the runway the first time Lieutenant Glassburn took the P-36A aloft loomed large in his sight as the radial-engine Curtiss fighter tugged to the left, got airborne, and flew over the heads of the men. Airborne in a fighter! Then it was time to clean up the typical Curtiss landing gear and get used to the P-36.[160]

The P-36 gave way to its long-nosed sibling, a P-40E. "It didn't seem like much of a transition at all," Ken said. Between his arrival at Hamilton Field in August and his hurried outbound convoy ride to the Pacific in November, Ken Glassburn only fired the P-40's machine guns once, at no target, out over the Pacific Ocean so he could check that requirement off. "We flew probably 10 to 15 times at Hamilton before we shipped over." He was expected to be a fighter pilot in the best AAF pursuit of the day, yet Glassburn says he did not do many aerobatics at Hamilton. "They didn't give us a lot of training; very little in combat maneuvers," he added.

Deteriorating political realities in the Pacific made it prudent to upgrade and reinforce American airpower in the Philippines by the late fall of 1941. Half of Glassburn's 21st Pursuit Squadron

The wing of the P-40 was mated as a single unit to the fuselage. The engine bay shows no wasted space, with V-1710 powerplant, accessories, and engine mount snugly packed together. *SDAM*

departed Hamilton in November, followed by Glassburn and the rest of the squadron later that month. Glassburn's convoy left San Francisco on Thanksgiving 1941, reaching Oahu by about the first of December. He was well out to sea when Pearl Harbor was attacked. Second Lieutenant Glassburn and a small contingent of 21st Pursuit Squadron personnel, along with many foot soldiers, arrived in Australia. "We were the first troops to land in Australia after the war started. That was two days before Christmas." The need for P-40s for combat was urgent. Glassburn and his 35th Pursuit Group compatriots were rushed to the Amberley Erection Depot at Ipswich, Australia, where they helped build up P-40Es that arrived in crates. "I was putting on wings and everything else," he explained. "We'd put 10 airplanes together and get them tested and put 10 pilots together and send them out." Some of these quickly assembled Warhawks became the tools of brave fliers fighting the losing battle over Java in early 1942.[161]

After seeing several batches of P-40s off to war, Glassburn was tapped to take a P-40E into the fray as a last-ditch effort to reinforce the garrison at Java. His was one of more than 30 Warhawks intended to be flown to Melbourne, for shipment aboard the U.S.S. *Langley* to Java. On the ferry flight, north of Sydney, Glassburn's new P-40 began spewing oil that soon coated the windscreen. As the rest of his flight landed on the gravel runway at Williamston, Glassburn circled overhead. When they were accounted for on the ground, Lieutenant Glassburn came in for a landing, sideslipping the olive-drab Curtiss to provide better visibility than the murky windscreen offered. "My airspeed was a little high and I hit a bump in the middle of the runway." The long-nosed Warhawk turned a somersault in a shower of gravel, coming to rest inverted. Ken felt the pain of a broken arm as he scrambled to extricate himself from the upset fighter. Reaching for his safety harness, the fact that he was inverted in his seat was momentarily lost on Ken—until he released the latch and dropped unceremoniously on his head. "I had a couple stitches in the top of my head," he laughed later.[162]

While Lieutenant Glassburn recovered in the hospital, his squadron mates took the rest of the P-40s on to the *Langley*. En route to Java, Japanese aircraft found and sank the *Langley* on 27 February 1942; when most of the pilots were safely aboard another ship, it too was sunk. The fateful landing mishap in Australia that broke Ken Glassburn's arm may have saved his life. His days as a P-40 pilot were over; once out of the hospital, he was needed to fly C-47s, first in New Guinea, then elsewhere. But fate and fame were not through with Ken Glassburn yet—on 6 June 1944, after delivering paratroops to France in the Normandy invasion, Ken's C-47 caught fire from bullet damage. He set it down in the English Channel, where he and his crew were picked up by a British naval vessel, from which they watched the rest of the greatest invasion in history.

And how did Ken Glassburn assess the P-40 when he was introduced to it back in 1941? "We thought it was the best in the world."

Flight Lieutenant M. T. Vanderpump, RNZAF

Presentation of the U.S. Distinguished Flying Cross to Flight Lieutenant Vanderpump at Espiritu Santos followed his three tours of duty in the Pacific, including a 17 December mission in which he maneuvered his Warhawk on a fighter sweep over Rabaul following a 240-mile navigation over open sea. Flying into a superior number of Zeros, Vanderpump led his section of Curtiss fighters in an aggressive attack only hundreds of feet over the Japanese airfield.[163]

After dispatching one of the Japanese fighters, Vanderpump saw the other pilot in his subsection

Following heroic action over Rabaul, RNZAF F/Lt. M.T.Vanderpump received an American Distinguished Flying Cross in outdoor ceremonies at Espiritu Santo. *Air Force*

under attack by another enemy interceptor, which Vanderpump challenged and shot down. Now the object of attack by eight Japanese fighters, Vanderpump fought down to surface level while looking for his subsection fellow Warhawk flier to no avail; the other RNZAF pilot later was presumed shot down during that melee.[164]

Vanderpump's .50-caliber machine guns fell silent as he expended his ammunition, forcing him to head for home, under constant attack. According to the USAAF, "He was only able to escape from his unfavorable situation by a feat of skillful and audacious airmanship which involved flying over broken country at tree-top height, and over the heavily defended base at Rabaul at roof-top level." Evasive maneuvering is much more demanding than merely sitting in the cockpit of an aircraft; every wrenching bank slams the pilot side to side as his body pays the price for coming up against the laws of physics governing inertia. Every violent pitch-up prompts an almost unconscious tightening of abdominal muscles to support G-induced weight factors, and to keep oxygen and blood coursing through the body, as they must. It is a grunting, straining effort to stay alive, to stay one thought ahead of an adversary in a comparable machine. Vanderpump's rugged Curtiss fighter was the subject of attacks until he was well out over the trackless sea. His successful return home in a damaged Warhawk was cause for cheer, and, according to the USAAF, his "fearless determination to attack the enemy regardless of the odds" and his "unfailing cheerfulness" and piloting skill were only some of the reasons he was honored with the American Distinguished Flying Cross.[165]

Gene R. Chase, Rain Maker

Northwestern Nebraska is a broad, bountiful agricultural asset served by the meandering North Platte River and regularly shadowed by towering cumulonimbus clouds that can bring nurturing rain—or hurl crop-demolishing hailstones. Crop

The Nebraska weather modification P-40N flown by Gene Chase in 1956 carried a white radar pod beneath the right wing. *Gene R. Chase*

This P-40E, without gunsight in the top cutout of the instrument panel, shows the arrangement of instruments for the pilot's use. Flight instruments (airspeed, altitude, heading) are mostly clustered inside the painted outline in the left-center location; engine performance instruments are grouped to the right of this. *Air Force via Bowers collection*

duster Jim Cook, frustrated at having his Stearman biplane damaged by hail every season, applied science and entrepreneurialism to challenge nature. He knew a vapor of silver iodide, wafted into a budding storm cloud at the right time, could attract moisture out of the cloud before it could condense and freeze as hail, and fall instead as harmless raindrops.

Cook talked about his idea to all who would listen in Scottsbluff, Nebraska—local farmers, the Rotary Club, anyone he could enlist to support his idea of cloud-seeding to manage hail. In July 1954, he tried a twin-engine Douglas A-20 as a hail-suppression aircraft; by September 1954, Cook brought a surplus P-40M to Scottsbluff to begin the work of seeding nascent storm clouds. It worked, and Cook sought a seeding aircraft with higher performance, next using a former racing Mustang. When the U.S. Weather Service hired Cook to perform tornado research flights near Kansas City, the Scottsbluff hail suppression program was a fruit to be plucked by the Weather Modification Company of San Jose, California.

From its stable of Warhawks, Weather Modification furnished a gray P-40N (N1197N), replete with the obligatory sharkmouth, as well as a radar van staffed by a technician who doubled as a mechanic for some of the Warhawk's needs. From the local population in 1956, Gene Chase, a natural gas utility company engineer who also flew

The rainmaking chemical dispenser on the left side of the aft fuselage enabled this P-40N to draw moisture from storms before it had the chance to freeze and fall as damaging hail. *Gene R. Chase*

F8F Bearcats in Colorado as a weekend warrior, hired on to fly the P-40, taking vacation hours from his regular job whenever brewing storms dictated. Another local pilot, Bob Drainey, took the night shift—hail doesn't form only in daylight hours. From the start, the operation had its externally imposed quirks. Wyoming, a scant 20 air miles away, forbade cloud-seeding, so the ground radar operator did double duty, locating storm conditions and keeping an eye on Gene's path to steer him clear of the neighboring state. Eventually, Gene said, some locals who thought weather intervention was wrong persuaded Nebraska to ban the operations, after Chase had left the company.

He recalled the Scottsbluff Airport was a surplus bomber training base with three runways of about 8,000 feet in length. Prevailing surface winds during hail season in northwest Nebraska were southeasterly, so Chase and his fellows took to parking the P-40 at the appropriate end of the runway "so all we had to do is hop in and take off," without taxiing a mile and a half in the hot sun first. "A long taxi in hot weather doesn't do any of them (liquid-cooled warbirds) any good," Gene added.

The secrets of the cloud-seeding P-40's successes were a propane tank and burner, a silver iodide supply that was vaporized by the burner, and a radar pod under the Warhawk's right wing, with a scope in the cockpit telling Gene where it was already raining, and hence where he did not need to fly. Backed up by the ground radar set, Chase would launch into the humid Nebraska sky when forming clouds threatened to mushroom into full-blown storms. As the storms built, their sometimes-violent circulating air currents created updrafts and downdrafts. Left to nature, these drafts could carry moist air up to freezing level, where hail would plummet to earth with damaging consequences to crops. Chase's tactic was to fly in the vicinity of an updraft where the release of silver iodide vapor would result in the production of rain, not hail, before the moisture could get high enough. Starting at Scottsbluff's field elevation—3,945 feet—he would typically climb another 2,000 feet or so above the terrain. "I tried to stay at the base of the clouds and not get in them," he explained, but sometimes the same updraft that sucked the silver iodide vapor skyward pulled the sturdy P-40 into its lightning-spangled maw. Luckily, he brought his Navy Reserve flight gear—including a hard-shell flying helmet—with him when he rattled around in the P-40 in storms. The ferocity of the turbulent storms sent a healthy jolt of adrenaline coursing through Gene's system a time or two, he recalled, and his best maneuver when caught in an updraft was to "throttle back and drop down out of it" in the heavy Warhawk. Typically Chase flew the P-40 at 140 miles per hour indicated airspeed because "I didn't want to beat the airplane up in rough air" at higher speeds.

To begin the seeding operation, Chase first opened a valve that released propane from its tank, and then he switched an electric ignition device to fire the propane. Into this he released silver iodide. The seeding device was visible outside the left aft fuselage section of the P-40N. "As I recall, each flight lasted about one hour," he explained. In addition to the rigors of storm flying, Gene Chase had other escapades in the working Warhawk. Asked if he ever performed aerobatics in the hail fighter, he acknowledged, "yeah, but the company never knew it." And then Gene, the Navy-trained fighter pilot, only flew gentle loops and rolls "without stressing the airplane." "It was easy to fly," he added; only the narrow track of the main gear gave any cause for concern on landing. Where some P-40 pilots found it difficult to keep the plane rolling straight in three-point, tail-low landings as prescribed by Curtiss, Gene said he never gave that a thought. He always landed three-point; "we were never taught to make a wheel landing (on the main gear first) in the Navy," he explained.

A generator failure in instrument conditions cut all electrical power to the P-40 once, and brought the best of Gene's training into play. His first clue was when the old monochrome radar scope went blank. Remembering the Curtiss Electric propeller's trait of going into high pitch when electrical power was lost, Gene quickly intervened and selected manual pitch control before that happened. Heading back to the Scottsbluff runway, he lowered the landing gear while the electrically pumped hydraulic system still had enough battery power to ensure the gear would go down and lock in place. Then, on final approach, Chase found he still had enough battery power to lower the flaps for landing.

Generally, parts and maintenance were not problems for the Scottsbluff P-40 operation. When the generator failed, a phone call to the company home base in California brought a spare generator winging back to Scottsbluff aboard Weather Modification's own P-38, Chase said. "The radar man and I put it on the P-40," he added. High-octane 110/130 aviation gasoline was available at Scottsbluff, thanks to the needs of scheduled airliners that also served the airport.

Near the end of Gene Chase's tenure with Weather Modification flights, another pilot took the P-40 to Denver for some needed radio repairs beyond the scope of anyone in Scottsbluff. The Warhawk came to grief in a belly landing in Colorado in 1956, Gene remembered. In an era before P-40s were valued as icons, it was relegated to a boneyard there for some time. Eventually, at least portions of it came back to life at Ed Maloney's Planes of Fame Museum at Chino, California. Gene finished out the season in an AT-6 furnished by Weather Modification Company, and then moved on to other endeavors, including a long-standing affiliation with the Experimental Aircraft Association and its annual show at Oshkosh, Wisconsin.

And what does Gene Chase think about the P-40 more than four decades after he flew it? "My recollections of flying that airplane are fond," he said. "I'd like to hop another one sometime."[166]

Civilian P-40s

Large numbers of P-40s survived the war as trainers in the United States. While many were unceremoniously parted from their engines and stacked tail-up on their firewalls, awaiting final scrapping, others filtered into the peacetime civilian market.

Canadian P-40s, mostly E-model equivalents, were bought and returned to the United States in the late 1940s, chiefly out of Boeing Field in Seattle, Washington.

It is from these Canadian stocks that one of the most remarkable survivors emanated. It was mounted atop a small gas station for decades in Everett, Washington, before being gingerly lifted off and restored to flying condition. As a Royal Canadian Air Force (RCAF) aircraft, it bore the Canadian serial number AK899. Bought surplus in 1947 by Fred Dyson, this Kittyhawk became a huge red sign ornament on a Flying-A gasoline station in the lumber and port town of Everett, Washington, some 40 miles north of Seattle. Popular lore had it that each time the gas station got a

The second XP-40Q had a short-lived air racing career. It caught fire during the 1947 Thompson Trophy event. *Bodie/SDAM*

Like a ghost, this bare metal P-40E in Canadian civil registration (CF-OGZ) appeared at the growing Abbotsford International Air Show one summer in the first half of the 1960s. The aircraft was, at the time, registered to an owner in Calgary, Alberta. Subsequently it flew under two U.S. registration numbers, N11122 and N40PE. *Jim Larsen*

new coat of paint, so did the P-40, thereby mummifying its aluminum against the ravages of coastal air. By the early 1970s, the red Curtiss had been sold and taken down from the vintage gas station to begin a new career with Yesterday's Air Force in Chino, California. Restored with a basic olive and gray USAAF scheme, *sans* sharkmouth, old AK899 (with U.S. civil registration N9837A) made a number of air show appearances including some venues not far from its former perch in Everett. From Yesterday's Air Force to Military Aircraft Restoration Group, the born-again P-40 was next acquired by Richard W. Hansen in Illinois.

Another Canadian with a charmed life is E-model 41-13574 (ex-RCAF number 1047), which passed from Fred Dyson's ownership after the war through a series of private owners in the eastern and southern United States before coming to rest under the aegis of the Boy Scouts in Meridian, Mississippi, by 1952. Twelve years later, this P-40E became the example in the National Air and Space Museum (NASM) of the Smithsonian Institution in Washington, D.C.[167]

Working Warbirds

While many civilian P-40s were used for recreational or business transportation, several earned their keep as weather-modification—cloud-seeding—aircraft. (See also chapter 7.) The Weather Modification Company of Redlands and San Jose, California, acquired P-40E (ex-RCAF AK827) in about 1954 after it had passed through several owners, including Warhawk guardian angel Fred Dyson. After about 1957, this E-model again became the property of a succession of owners. At various times it has carried U.S. civil numbers N1223N and N40245.

The Weather Modification Company also obtained a P-40M (U.S. civil registration N1228N) in the mid-1950s; it was reported to have crashed

Blocking the horizon like a stand of midwest corn, upended engineless P-40s at Walnut Ridge, Arkansas, awaited smelting in the 1940s. *National Archives*

with a subsequent owner in the mid-1960s.

P-40M (43-5795, N1232N), also part of the Canadian migration to Seattle, became a Weather Modification Company mount in about 1957. Visitors to the old Harrah's automobile museum in Sparks, Nevada, later saw this same P-40 on display in the 1960s and into the early 1980s before it was acquired by warbird and air race enthusiast Bill Destefani in California's San Joaquin Valley.

A P-40N-5 (42-105192), from Canadian surplus, later became Weather Modification's N1197N in about 1956. After a mishap in Colorado in the 1950s, it went to Ed Maloney's warbird collection, and became the Planes of Fame Museum's N85104.

Off to the Races

It's difficult to imagine a P-40 as a serious air racing contender in a postwar sky filled with fast P-51s and P-63s. But Skip Ziegler figured he had a chance with a surplus bubble-top P-40Q, the speedster that topped out at 422 miles per hour at 20,000 feet. Even though his clean and curious-looking P-40 (registration number NX300B) had not qualified for the 1947 Thompson trophy race, Ziegler took it up anyway, adding to the variety and spectacle until the beefy Allison V-1710 balked under the strain during the race's 13th lap. Ziegler swapped speed for altitude as he nosed the silver P-40Q skyward to give room for him to bail out. He sustained a broken leg; the P-40Q ignited a blaze in a railroad yard where it crashed.

Another effort to speed up a civilian P-40 resulted in a cut-down hybrid with a jet canopy. P-40N 44-7619 had been a surplus fixture of the high school at Chowchilla in California's bountiful San Joaquin Valley in the early 1950s. Going through subsequent owners, the N-model at some point acquired its cut-down canopy and clipped wingtips; the aesthetics were somewhat clever, but this heavy P-40N, then registered as N1251N, was not to be a serious racing contender.

Interruption of the National Air Races thwarted the project, which lay dormant for part of the 1950s. Ed Maloney secured the modified Warhawk and reverted it to stock configuration. Subsequently, former WASP Suzanne Parrish campaigned this aircraft in a somewhat stylized version of desert pink camouflage and re-registered N222SU; the aircraft is displayed as of this writing in the Kalamazoo Air Museum in Michigan.

P-40s have figured in motion pictures since John Wayne mounted wartime movie mockups for the film *Flying Tigers*. Decades later, when major studios were taking advantage of available warbirds to lend splendor to their films, two P-40Es were shipped to Hawaii to fly for the cameras in *Tora! Tora! Tora!* Perhaps more remarkable than the two flying Warhawks over Hawaii were the rows of accurate-looking fiberglass replica P-40Es demolished in the movie's air raid sequences. Cast from a genuine fuselage, the non-flying replicas used Beech C-45 outer wing panels in a clever amalgamation. Some could be taxied to add to the sense of realism. As of this writing, one of the fiberglass survivors of filming was displayed at Wheeler Field on Oahu.

Tomahawk Revival

Just when enthusiasts despaired of ever seeing an early Tomahawk variant, a group calling itself Project Tomahawk set up shop at the airport at Compton, California. In the southern California ambiance of customized cars and movie magic, nothing seems impossible, and Project Tomahawk is forging ahead with a scratchbuilt Tomahawk, to be powered by an early Allison of the right configuration.

Even as the new Tomahawk was taking form in California, the breakdown of the rigid Soviet Union

continued on page 105

Gil Macy's P-40E with a modified canopy and a four-blade propeller was joined in flight over western Washington by a black-and-gold F8F Bearcat in the summer of 1967, when military paint schemes on surplus aircraft were not yet in ascendancy. This Warhawk, N151U, went through several civil registration numbers in subsequent years, and was restored to its original appearance, at one time being the mascot of Flying Tiger Airlines. It formerly served in the Royal Canadian Air Force as serial number AK979. *Jim Larsen*

When Max Hoffman owned ex-RCAF P-40E AK905, the aircraft was banked over south Texas farmland for the camera of Jim Larsen during a Confederate Air Force Warbird Air Show, circa 1976. This P-40 subsequently was acquired by Rudy Frasca, and is a perennial favorite at air shows including the EAA Fly-In Convention at Oshkosh, Wisconsin.

Color Gallery

The Royal New Zealand Air Force employed P-40s, including these N-models, in Pacific combat against the Japanese. *Leo M. Myers collection*

Over a brilliant watercolor explosion, desert-camouflaged P-40s bomb a German tank force in a Curtiss-Wright advertisement touting the ground attack capabilities of the Warhawk. *Don Keller collection*

Guns blazing, a new P-40N roars off the page in a wartime Curtiss advertisement depicting various models of the aircraft in combat around the world, including radial-engine export P-36A-derived Mohawks in Asia. *Don Keller collection*

Slumbering in a hilltop orchard above Troutdale, Oregon, on 23 April 1967 was the P-40M (43-5802) owned by Bob Sturges of Columbia Airmotive. Operated by the RCAF as number 840, this Warhawk passed through several postwar owners before coming to reside with Columbia Airmotive until about 1972. Subsequently sold and refurbished, this flyable P-40M went to the Fighter Collection in Duxford, U.K., in 1985. *Kenneth G. Johnsen*

P-40N in the Ontario Air Museum (now Planes of Fame) collection was photographed at Ontario, California, 24 March 1969. *Kenneth G. Johnsen*

Following stardom in the motion picture *Tora! Tora! Tora!*, this P-40E was parked in a hangar at Long Beach, California, when photographed 16 September 1969. Cast-fiberglass replica P-40s filled the *Tora! Tora! Tora!* flightline sequences in Hawaii. *Kenneth G. Johnsen*

For many years until removed from display, this P-40N was part of the aviation collection at Traveltown, a transportation museum in Griffith Park, Los Angeles, California. (See also photo on page 104.) *Garry Pape collection*

P-40E (RCAF AL152) was in the spotlight after going through several owners when movie pilot Frank Tallman bought this Warhawk in 1958. When Tallmantz Aviation auctioned a number of aircraft after cofounder Paul Mantz' death, N1207V was reportedly sold for $7,000 in 1968. *Garry Pape collection*

TP-40N 44-47923 was a two-seater operated by the Tallmantz Motion Picture Aviation Company out of Orange County in California when photographed; as of this writing it is in the collection of Kermit Weeks in Florida. *Garry Pape collection*

A returning favorite at air shows like Oshkosh, Wisconsin, in 1996, is Rudy Frasca's P-40E (RCAF AK905) in Flying Tiger markings with Nationalist Chinese roundels. *Author photo*

Before the Harrah's transportation collection in Reno, Nevada, was downsized, it included aircraft like P-40M (ex-RCAF AK845), photographed on display in 1967. *Garry Pape collection*

A clever copy, this replica P-40N, made largely of fiberglass, greeted visitors to the March Field Museum at Riverside, California, when photographed in 1996. *Author photo*

Before military paint schemes were the norm, Gil Macy's modified P-40E nudged into that category with a sharkmouth that does the breed proud. It was the summer of 1967, over western Washington during air show season, when Macy's Warhawk paced the camera plane of noted aviation photographer Jim Larsen for this striking portrait. Later, this P-40 (N151U) received a standard canopy and three-blade propeller once more.

This P-40E, once fitted with a four-blade propeller and modified canopy for a second seat, was reverted to near-original appearance, although the ability to carry a passenger remained. For a period of time in the 1970s, the aircraft wore a representation of RAF camouflage and markings, as photographed over California. *Jim Larsen*

No aircraft ever accommodated the snarling sharkmouth device as aptly as the P-40, making this marking almost obligatory on surviving warbird examples. Photographed at the Experimental Aircraft Association (EAA) Oshkosh, Wisconsin, show in 1995 was Richard Hansen's N9837A, one of the ex-Canadian examples saved after the war. It survived by serving as a gas station ornament in Everett, Washington, when most other P-40s were scrapped. *Author photo*

The business end of a P-40E approaches the camera plane over cloud-dappled fields of south Texas, circa 1976, during the annual October Confederate Air Force Warbird Extravaganza. A raised carburetor scoop on the nose of Allison-powered Warhawks limited the pilot's view during deflection shooting in a turning dogfight. *Jim Larsen*

Suzanne Parrish of Kalamazoo, Michigan, flew this pink P-40N (44-7619) during the October 1977 Confederate Air Force Air Show at Harlingen, Texas. *Author photo*

Rich earthen British browns and tans accent the markings on this Merlin-powered P-40F in North Africa, circa early 1943. The yellow-rimmed star insignia appears on both sides of both wings, a practice common in North Africa during this period. The undersurface on this repossessed aircraft originally intended for Britain has a far bluer tint than American gray. *Peter M. Bowers collection*

First production model, this exhaust- and oil-smudged straight P-40 (no suffix letter), serial 39-184, helped new pilots make the jump from two-seat Texan trainers to single-seat fighters at Luke Field, Arizona, circa 1942. *Peter M. Bowers collection*

An ex-RCAF P-40E took up residence for about two decades atop a gas station in Everett, Washington, as photographed in the mid-1960s. Evidently, repeated painting of the gas station and its Kittyhawk ornament helped preserve the airframe against corrosion. Removed from its perch about 1973, this P-40 was shipped to southern California for rebuilding to airworthy status, registered N9837A. *Author photo*

The former gas station Kittyhawk posed for an inflight portrait during an air show at Bellingham, Washington, in July 1980, with Bud Granley at the controls. It was subsequently operated by Richard W. Hansen of Batavia, Illinois. *Author photo*

The Champlin Fighter Museum, Mesa, Arizona, showed its P-40N (44-7192) in Nationalist Chinese livery when photographed in 1990. This is the former Traveltown/Griffith Park static display Warhawk. *Jim Morrow*

Richard Hansen's former gas station mascot Kittyhawk (N9837A) was part of a record-setting number of warbirds flying during the 1995 Experimental Aircraft Association show at Oshkosh, Wisconsin. *Author photo*

With a red rising sun not perfectly masking the star beneath it, this captured P-40E languished in Japan at war's end when American pilots discovered it. Though the Japanese learned about the performance of the Warhawk from captured examples, their one-time plan of using them for home defense evidently did not materialize. *Weir/Tom Foote collection*

continued from page 95
allowed capitalistic inroads to be made into this huge geographical warehouse of forgotten World War II warplanes. In the 1990s, a former Soviet P-40 Tomahawk subsequently arrived at Fighter Rebuilders in Chino, California, for restoration. Money and the desire to resurrect the lines of the earliest P-40s have allowed a style of P-40s once thought extinct to be returned from the grave.

Two long-body P-40Ns step back in echelon formation behind P-40E NX40PE over Harlingen, Texas, circa October 1976. N-model number "40" is a P-40N-30 (44-7369). Airworthy Warhawks of several models continue to perform in the United States and abroad. *Jim Larsen*

This trio of tigers over south Texas circa 1976 calls to mind the Flying Tigers over rural China, in search of Japanese bombers and fighters. Continually appreciating values of warbirds have provided incentive to breathe life into once-derelict airframes. An ever-more-sophisticated fraternity of warbird pilots and owners is taking steps to ensure the longevity of aircraft like the P-40. *Jim Larsen*

Bud Granley flew Dave Tallichet's P-40E during the Bellingham, Washington, air show in the summer of 1980. One of the most remarkable warbird rebirths of all, this fighter previously slumbered atop a gas station in Everett, Washington, for many years before it was taken down and refurbished for flight. It is former RCAF number AK899, later registered N9837A, and was subsequently sold to Richard W. Hansen. *Frederick A. Johnsen*

The Tomahawk could eject flares from a door in the wing undersurface, as photographed on a restoration project at Chino, California, in 1995. *Author photo*

At Torrance, California, an ambitious tribute to the P-40 design is this handbuilt Tomahawk (photographed in 1995) in a jig, using some original parts like the engine mount. Supporters of Project Tomahawk embarked on this remarkable undertaking to build a flyable aircraft. *Author photo*

(LEFT) This Tomahawk wing under restoration shows how the P-40 wheel well was circular to accommodate a tire; the main strut rested outside the wing's surface when it retracted, perhaps indicative of the wing's adaptation from the earlier fixed-gear P-36. *Author photo*

USAAF P-40 Combat Units and International Users

The P-40's longevity in production made it a ubiquitous presence in the Army Air Forces during World War II. Many fighter units used P-40s in combat at some time, while others used the Warhawk as the great stepping stone between AT-6 trainers and even higher-powered combat fighters for new fliers. So pervasive was the P-40, it may be impossible to tally every AAF organization that ever operated them, but known combat units that had P-40s include:

8th Fighter Group; included P-40s in its arsenal before World War II and then again in 1943 and into early 1944 while assigned to theFifth Air Force for combat.

8th Reconnaissance Group; had P-40s along with

The straight P-40s were the only fighters delivered in a markings combination that included stars on both wings, rudder stripes, and camouflage. This example hit the dirt in an oilfield at Coalinga, California, in March 1941. It was assigned to the 20th Pursuit Group, as shown by the "20P" on the vertical fin. The hand of cards painted on the fuselage is the emblem of the 77th Pursuit Squadron, which was operating out of Moffett Field, California, at the time it was photographed. *Air Force via Ben Howser collection*

To commemorate building 15,000 fighters of all types, Curtiss painted the Warhawk that corresponded to that number with the insignia of all the countries that had operated Curtiss pursuits. The P-40N's wide use as a ground-attack airplane was highlighted by three shackled bombs on the commemorative plane, with red noses, white middles, blue afterbodies, and red tailfins. The obligatory sharkmouth was given more than the usual paint treatment, with shadow shading added for dramatic effect. Rudder stripes were red and white, with a blue vertical stripe. The bands around the forward fuselage ahead of the cockpit were red at the front, followed by white and blue. The legend "15,000th Curtiss Fighter" on the nose was yellow. The propeller spinner was red. *Curtiss/SDAM*

other types in India beginning in early 1944. This unit flew some escort and strafing missions.

14th Fighter Group; trained with P-40s and P-43s in prewar 1941 and then converted to P-38s after Pearl Harbor was bombed.

15th Fighter Group; contributed P-40s to the defense of Pearl Harbor on 7 December 1941.

16th Fighter Group; equipped with P-40s in 1941, the unit was disbanded in the Canal Zone on 1 November 1943.

18th Fighter Group; had recently converted to P-40s on Oahu when Pearl Harbor was attacked, sustaining heavy losses. Switched to other types of fighters circa 1943.

20th Fighter Group; used P-40s and P-39s in the U.S. for air defense early in the war, later becoming a P-38 unit in Eighth Air Force.

23rd Fighter Group; assumed role previously performed by Chennault's Flying Tigers in China, using P-40s and then P-51s.

24th Pursuit Group; as the entire pursuit force available in the Philippines in December 1941, this unit included P-40s, and detailed squadrons, in its complement.

27th Fighter Group; converted to P-40s in January 1944 while already in Mediterranean Theater combat, acquiring P-47s a half year later.

28th Composite (after December 1943, **28th Bombardment**) **Group**; numbered P-40s in its varied inventory between 1941–43 in Alaska.

32nd Fighter Group; used P-40s and other fighters, including P-36s, P-39s, and P-26s, for training and in defense of the Panama Canal, where it disbanded on 1 November 1943.

Captured booty, this former Soviet P-40M subsequently flew in Finnish markings. *Peter M. Bowers collection*

33rd Fighter Group; after starting training in P-39s in 1941, the unit switched to P-40s; performed air defense along east coast of United States in 1942 before moving with P-40s to North Africa later that year.

35th Fighter Group; trained with aircraft including P-40s before the war; sent some P-40s to the Philippines to augment 24th Pursuit Group.

36th Fighter Group; flew P-40s and P-39s from Puerto Rico, 1941–43, as air defense for the Caribbean and Panama Canal.

37th Fighter Group; used P-40s to replace ancient P-26s for Panama Canal defenses; disbanded there on 1 November 1943.

48th Fighter Group; had some P-40s among diverse warplanes between 1942 and 1944 as a replacement training unit stateside, with additional duties, before becoming a 9th Air Force P-47 outfit.

49th Fighter Group; acquired P-40s in Australia in 1942, providing active air defense there before moving to New Guinea that October.

50th Fighter Group; used some P-40s stateside as part of the Fighter Command School and later AAF School of Applied Tactics, then moved to England in 1944 to become a 9th Air Force Thunderbolt group.

51st Fighter Group; assigned to stateside 4th Air Force with P-40s in 1941, then to 10th Air Force in India in March 1942, defending Indian terminus of the Hump supply route.

52nd Fighter Group; trained with P-39s and P-40s and participated in stateside maneuvers, 1941 to mid-1942, when it moved to England and converted to Spitfires in 8th Air Force.

53rd Fighter Group; trained with P-40s and P-35s before the war, then equipped with P-39s for air defense of the Canal Zone in December 1941.

54th Fighter Group; trained with P-40s in 1941, the following year switching to P-39s.

56th Fighter Group; equipped with P-40s and P-39s in 1941, flying maneuvers and later air defense missions in the southern and eastern U.S. before converting with P-47s in June 1942 for subsequent 8th Air Force combat.

57th Fighter Group; trained with P-40s in 1941, served as East Coast Air Defense Unit until relocating to the Middle East for operations in the summer of 1942, beginning combat there in October.

58th Fighter Group; used P-35s, P-36s, P-39s, and P-40s as a replacement training unit, later preparing for Pacific combat with P-47s and becoming a Fifth Air Force group.

59th Fighter Group; a part of this stateside pilot-training group received P-40s a month before the unit disbanded in Thomasville, Georgia, on 1 May 1944.

66th Tactical Reconnaissance Group; included some P-40s in its varied lineup used to support stateside Army ground units on maneuvers.

68th Reconnaissance Group; included P-40s in its Mediterranean operations.

69th Reconnaissance Group; had many types of aircraft, including P-40s, engaged in Pacific coast patrols and air-ground training.

71st Reconnaissance Group; used some P-40s while in the United States, before converting to other types for southwest Pacific combat in the fall of 1943.

74th Reconnaissance Group; had P-40s among its nine aircraft varieties sometime between 1942 and 1945, for stateside support of maneuvers.

75th Reconnaissance Group; included P-40s for ground support training and replacement training.

76th Reconnaissance Group; had some P-40s for working with ground units in the United States.

77th Reconnaissance Group; numbered P-40s in its roster for providing reconnaissance support to ground units in training in the United States; may have flown patrols along the Mexican border in part of 1942 with P-40s.

79th Fighter Group; trained with P-40s in late 1942 and into 1943 while already in the Middle East, entering combat with Warhawks as a 9th AF unit.

This Turkish Tomahawk IIB came from a batch originally meant for Great Britain. *Bowers collection*

80th Fighter Group; began operations in September 1943 with P-40s and P-38s as a 10th Air Force outfit in India, subsequently converting to P-47s.

81st Fighter Group; following P-39 operations in the Middle East, this group moved to India in the spring of 1944 and began training with P-40s and P-47s before moving to China that May as part of 14th Air Force.

85th Fighter Group; received P-40s and a few P-47s early in 1944 to replace A-36s when this unit was a replacement training group in the United States.

86th Fighter Group; included P-40s in its combat array in the Mediterranean in 1943 and possibly into 1944 as a 12th Air Force asset.

312th Bombardment Group; as a light or dive-bomb group at different times, had P-40s in training and then flew combat patrols and escort missions with P-40s in New Guinea in late 1943 and early 1944 before converting to A-20s by February.

318th Fighter Group; activated in Hawaii in October 1942, the group used P-40s, P-39s, and P-47s for Hawaiian patrols before moving to the Marianas in June 1944.

324th Fighter Group; moved to the Middle East in fall and winter of 1942, continued training with P-40s, beginning operations against Axis in Tunisia as a unit of the 9th Air Force. Moved into Italy; switched to P-47s in July 1944.

325th Fighter Group; trained with P-40s, moving to North Africa in early 1943 with 12th Air Force.

327th Fighter Group; performed air defense and operational training as a First Air Force group from late summer of 1942 until February 1943 when P-47s were received.

332nd Fighter Group; trained with P-40s and P-39s circa late 1942 and 1943, before entering combat in Italy.

337th Fighter Group; used P-40s in 1942–43 as a Third Air Force replacement training group.

338th Fighter Group; included P-40s in its fleet for training replacement crews as a Third Air Force group during the last half of 1942 and into 1943.

342nd Composite Group; activated 11 September 1942 in Iceland, this unit included some P-40s as part of the air defense for the region.

The four guns buried in the wings shows this to be an RAF Kittyhawk I, equivalent to the P-40D. *Curtiss via Peter M. Bowers*

Common as a trainer, a long line of Warhawks basks on the flightline under puffy June clouds at Thomasville, Georgia, in 1945. For many fighter pilots, the Warhawk was the first leap from two-seat trainers to a high-performance single-seat combat type. *Air Force*

343rd Fighter Group; used P-40s and P-38s in combat over the Aleutians beginning September 1942, flying its last combat in October 1943.

369th Fighter Group; included some P-40s to train replacement crews and participate in maneuvers in 1943–44 as part of the Third, and later Fourth, Air Force.

372nd Fighter Group; from late 1943 until June 1945, this stateside training and support unit primarily relied on P-40s until converting to P-51s in June 1945.

408th Fighter-Bomber Group; trained in the United States with aircraft including P-40s, A-24s, A-26s, and P-47s.

International Users

The British Royal Air Force, while the major foreign user of P-40s, was by no means the only other nation to take these Curtiss fighters to war. (In fact, Japan at one time gave serious consideration to employing P-40Es captured in Java as home defense fighters, but stopped short of doing so in part because the P-40's rate of climb was inferior to available Japanese types.) British Commonwealth and aligned countries flew P-40s. These included:

Australia: One hundred sixty-three P-40E-1s, actually Kittyhawk IA variants, were sent to Australia. Inexperienced but doughty fliers took Royal Australian Air Force (RAAF) Kittyhawks to a field near Port Moresby to begin challenging the Japanese in 1942. Other Australian P-40 pilots (No. 3 Squadron) bolstered the RAF effort in North Africa. When fighting around Salerno demanded ground support, innovative and daring RAAF P-40 pilots in the Mediterranean Theater of Operations landed at a recently deserted Italian airfield near the fighting, where their maintenance men arrived by transport in time to service the Curtisses and launch them for a mission with more fuel—hence time over target—than they could possibly have managed from their home field. M-models also served with Australia, and 468 P-40Ns were routed for Australian use. RAAF 80 Squadron flew P-40Ns from Noemfoor by 1944.

Brazil: Brazil received 6 P-40E-1s, followed by 25 K-models and 19 P-40Ms. Forty-one P-40Ns were sent to Brazil; they were re-serialled in 1945, and some remained in Brazilian service as late as 1958. One Brazilian P-40N was placed on display there.

Nationalist China operated Warhawks, including this P-40N. *Bowers collection*

Canada: Canadians initially used three former RAF Tomahawk Is (Model H81-A), still bearing their former British serials (AH774, AG793, and AH840), as instructional airframes. One Tomahawk IIA (AH938) likewise was transferred to Canada. Seventy-two Kittyhawk equivalents to P-40Ds, part of a batch originally intended for France and subsequently picked up by Britain, went to Canada, followed by Kittyhawk IAs. These were six-gun P-40E-1s (the -1 distinguished them as British export models). By 1942, Canadian P-40 squadrons were in the United Kingdom to support ground units if needed. That year, RCAF Kittyhawks flew alongside USAAF counterparts in defense of the Aleutians. RCAF squadrons serving in the Aleutians included numbers 14 (which added the familiar sharkmouth to their E-models) and 111. One RCAF P-40 pilot, the commander of 111 Squadron, was credited with downing a Zero on 25 September 1942. Nine P-40Ks with U.S. serials were flown by Canadians.[168]

Of the few P-40Ms extant as of this writing, two are from Canadian surplus. Kittyhawk IVs (P-40Ns) from RCAF stocks also entered the civilian market after the war; Canada at one time had at least 35 P-40Ns. One of the RCAF N-models (subsequently flown by the Planes of Fame museum in Chino, California) was supposed to have downed a Japanese incendiary balloon on 10 March 1945 over British Columbia.[169]

Other countries operated P-40s in some capacity; at least one Soviet example was captured by Finland during the war, and may have been used, in Finnish markings, against the Soviets. Other foreign users of P-40s included:

Egypt: The Egyptian Air Force was the recipient of some Tomahawk IIBs, about which little has been documented.

France: The first foreign customer for P-40s, France initially signed up for Model 81 Tomahawks (as the British subsequently christened them). The first French variant was ready by April 1940, but these were undeliverable with the fall of France, and Great Britain took over this batch. Instead, the first new P-40s received by Free French forces were Merlin-powered P-40Fs that were part of a batch of Kittyhawk IIs intended for Great Britain.[170]

Free French fliers of the Lafayette Groupe, many of them veterans of French P-36s, began operating P-40s in North Africa. Exposed to the hazards of ground attack, the French pilots in North Africa lost many of their Merlin-powered P-40s, although they did score several victories against Luftwaffe FW-190s and Ju-88s. French P-40s served until their retirement during the first half of postwar 1946.[171]

Nationalist China: The first P-40s to reach China were 100 Model 81s (sometimes referred to as H81-A3s. Chinese pilots flew Warhawks in combat against the Japanese as part of the China Air Task Force (see also chapters 3, 5, and 7 in this volume). Into the early postwar period, Chinese P-40Ns were in use.

The Netherlands: The last combat user of the P-40 was the Dutch Air Force, whose Warhawks were used against rebel forces in the Dutch East Indies as late as 1948 in a fight that ultimately saw the creation of Indonesia. In 1943, Dutch No. 120 Squadron was formed with P-40s and worked with the RAAF around Exmouth Gulf until the threat of a Japanese attack on Fremantle had passed. The squadron moved to Dutch New Guinea, flying ground attack missions, and thence to Noemfoor.

After the war, the 120st Squadron moved to Java. In December of 1948, the unit's last major air action with P-40s was in support of Dutch landings at Djocja. The next year these Dutch Warhawks were retired.[172]

New Zealand: P-40E-1s (Kittyhawk IAs) numbering 62 aircraft were consigned to New Zealand. P-40Ks and one L-model (New Zealand

This Packard-powered Kittyhawk II in British markings shows a hastily oversprayed fin flash on the vertical tail. *Peter M. Bowers collection*

A P-40N in British markings, this is a Kittyhawk IV. *Peter M. Bowers collection*

serial NZ3074) were received, and numerous P-40Ms flew for the Royal New Zealand Air Force. N-models also served New Zealand. Some seven squadrons of the RNZAF flew P-40s, the first beginning to do so in March 1942, some of the aircraft being hand-me-downs from the USAAF. Combat in the South Pacific included a mix of RNZAF P-40s.

South Africa: South African Air Force (SAAF) fliers took Tomahawk IIBs into combat beginning in June 1941. SAAF P-40 squadrons numbers 2, 4, 5, and 7 operated in the African desert, working up through Merlin-powered variants and K-models.

Soviet Union: Following allocation of 16 straight P-40s, the Soviet Union also received 23 Tomahawk IIAs and an equal number of IIBs. At least one Soviet Tomahawk squadron was positioned to provide defense for Moscow. Reports suggest some Soviet P-40s flew operationally with skis, an idea only tested by the USAAF. World War II Soviet pilots were frequently described by their American counterparts as bold, almost reckless in the degree to which they would wring performance out of Lend-Lease American equipment. Accounts of Soviet fighter pilots ramming German planes to score kills attest to the vigor with which they pursued their craft.[173] P-40Ms from British stocks also went to the Soviet Union. The last production version, the P-40N, included at least 130 for the Soviet Union.

Turkey: Tomahawk IIBs were the first of the Allison-engined Curtisses to wear the crescent and star insignia of Turkey on their rudders, with square Turkish national insignia on their wings.

Entering service in 1941, these 36 Tomahawks were assigned Turkish serial numbers 3801 through 3836, inclusive. Twenty-four (one source says 17) Kittyhawk Is, similar to four-gun P-40Ds, were also allocated to Turkey. Some Turkish P-40s—possibly the early Tomahawks—remained in the inventory as late as 1949. Turkey practiced neutrality during the war, sometimes shifting precariously in leaning toward or away from the Allies.[174]

RNZAF P-40 pilots from No. 17 Squadron gathered by the nose of one of their Curtisses at Espiritu Santo in November 1943. From left to right, Flight Lieutenant B. Thomson, Second Lieutenant P. G. H. Newton (RNZAF ace), and Flight Lieutenant A. Buchanan. When the photo was taken, No. 17 Squadron claimed nineteen enemy aircraft destroyed plus five probables. Nine of the kills and four probables occurred during a melee over Rabaul on Christmas Eve 1943. *Air Force*

Two RNZAF members at Guadalcanal in 1943 hold the trashed rudder from the Kittyhawk flown by Flight Officer Avery when attacked by Japanese fighters. *Air Force*

Betty was a P-40N in the Netherlands East Indies—the last holdout of combat Warhawks in the postwar 1940s. *Bowers collection*

Rhapsody in Rivets features a large snake head on the nose. Empty shackles and sway braces are silhouetted beneath the aircraft. *SDAM*

Appendices

Appendix 1

Curtiss P-40 USAAF Serial Numbers

The Air Corps, and later Army Air Forces, kept a master list of consecutive aircraft serial numbers that included the year of a contract followed by a specific serial number for each aircraft contained in that contract. By conducting the business of ordering warplanes this way, blocks of seemingly unrelated numbers came to represent the entire production run of aircraft like the P-40, since other contracts awarded to other manufacturers between P-40 batches would take up intervening consecutive serial numbers. The prefix letter "R" (as in RP-40) in this list was applied to some aircraft after they were no longer considered suitable for their original mission. Serial numbers allocated to the P-40 series are:

XP-40	38-010
RP-40	39-156 through 39-220
RP-40G	39-221
RP-40	39-222 through 39-289
RP-40	40-292 through 40-357
P-40E	40-358
RP-40D	40-359
XP-40F	40-360
RP-40D	40-361 through 40-381
P-40E	40-382 through 40-681
RP-40B	41-5205 through 41-5304
P-40E	41-5305 through 41-5744
RP-40B	41-13297 through 41-13327
RP-40C	41-13328 through 41-13520
P-40E	41-13521 through 41-13599
P-40F	41-13600 through 41-13695
P-40F	41-13697 through 41-14299
P-40F-5	41-14300 through 41-14422
P-40F-10	41-14423 through 41-14599
P-40F-15	41-19733 through 41-19932
P-40F-20	41-19933 through 41-20044
P-40E-1	41-24776 through 41-25195
P-40E-1	41-35874 through 41-36953
P-40K-5	42-9730 through 42-9929
P-40K-10	42-9930 through 42-10264
P-40K-15	42-10265 through 42-10429
P-40L-1	42-10430 through 42-10479
P-40L-5	42-10480 through 42-10699
P-40L-10	42-10700 through 42-10847
P-40L-15	42-10848 through 42-10959
P-40L-20	42-10960 through 42-11129
P-40K-1	42-45722 through 42-46321
P-40N-1	42-104429 through 42-104828
P-40N-5	42-104829 through 42-105928
P-40N-10	42-105929 through 42-106028
P-40N-15	42-106029 through 42-106405
P-40N-20	42-106406 through 42-106428
P-40M-1	43-5403 through 43-5462
P-40M-5	43-5463 through 43-5722
P-40M-10	43-5723 through 43-6002
P-40N-20	43-22752 through 43-24251
P-40N-25	43-24252 through 43-24570
XP-40Q	43-24571
P-40N-25	43-24572 through 43-24751
P-40N-30	44-7001 through 44-7500
P-40N-35	44-7501 through 44-8000
P-40N-40	44-47749 through 44-47968

Appendix 2

Comparison Data for Selected Aircraft Powered by Allison V-1710 Engines

Type and Model	Engine	Top Speed/ Altitude (mph/ft)	Service Ceiling (ft)	Range (miles)
XP-38	V-1710-11/15	413/20,000	38,000	
YP-38	V-1710-27/29	405/20,000	38,000	650 normal
P-38	"	390/20,000		825
P-38D	"	390/25,000	39,000	400 normal
P-38E	"	395/	39,000	500
P-38F	V-1710-49/53	395/25,000	39,000	
P-38J	V-1710-89/91	414/25,000	44,000	450
P-38L	V-1710-111/113	414/25,000	44,000	450
XP-39	V-1710-17	390/20,000	32,000	
XP-39B	V-1710-39	375/15,000	36,000	600 normal
YP-39	V-1710-37	368/13,600	33,300	600 normal
P-39C	V-1710-35	379/13,000	33,200	500 normal
P-39D/F/J	V-1710-35	368/13,800	32,100	800
XP-39E	V-1710-47	386/21,680	35,200	500 normal
P-39K/L	V-1710-63	368/13,800	32,000	800
P-39M	V-1710-83	386/9,500	36,000	650
P-39N	V-1710-85	399/9,700	38,500	750
P-39Q	V-1710-85	385/11,000	35,000	650
P-40	**V-1710-33**	**357/15,000**	**32,750**	**950**
P-40B	"	**352/15,000**	**32,400**	**940**
P-40E	**V-1710-39**	**354/15,000**	**29,000**	**700 normal**
P-40K	**V-1710-73**	**362/15,000**	**28,000**	**350**
P-40N-1	**V-1710-81**	**378/10,500**	**38,000**	**240**
XP-40Q	**V-1710-121**	**422/20,500**	**39,000**	
XP-51	V-1710-39	382/13,000	30,800	750 normal
P-51A	V-1710-81	390/20,000	31,350	"
A-36A	V-1710-87	366/5,000	27,000	550 w/bombs
P-63A	V-1710-95	408/24,450	43,000	450
P-63C	V-1710-117	410/25,000	38,600	320 w/bombs
P-63D	V-1710-109	437/30,000	39,000	950 w/bombs
F-82G	V-1710-143/145	461/21,000	38,900	2,240

Selected Aircraft Powered by Merlin Engines

Type and Model	Engine	Top Speed/ Altitude (mph/ft)	Service Ceiling (ft)	Range (miles)
P-40F	**V-1650-1**	**364/20,000**	**34,400**	**375**
P-51D	V-1650-7	437/25,000	41,900	950

NOTES: Aircraft performance statistics are somewhat academic, since combat aircraft in combat conditions can be different from test conditions. Range data listed here may vary depending on external tanks or bombs. The numbers do show trends in performance, and reveal marked improvements in Allison developments during World War II. Engine models for P-38s and the F-82G show both left and right engine numbers; all other aircraft are single engine.

Appendix 3

P-40 Aces

Col. John Alison (23rd Fighter Group) *6 Victories in P-40*
Lt. Col. Robert Baseler (325th Fighter Group) *5*
Maj. John G. Bright (AVG, later 23rd Fighter Group) *5*
Capt. Robert Byrne (57th Fighter Group) *6*
Maj. Levi R. Chase (33rd Fighter Group) *10*
Capt. Frank J. Collins (325th Fighter Group) *5*
Lt. Robert M. DeHaven (49th Fighter Group) *10*
Lt. I. B. Donalson (49th Fighter Group) *5*
Lt. Charles DuBois Jr. (23rd Fighter Group) *6*
2Lt. Richard E. Duffy (324th Fighter Group) *5*
Capt. Frank Gaunt (8th Fighter Group) *7*
Maj. Ed R. Goss (51st and 23rd Fighter Groups) *5*
Capt. William Grosvenor Jr. (23rd Fighter Group) *5*
Capt. John F. Hampshire (23rd Fighter Group) *13*
Capt. William J. Hennon (17th Pursuit Squadron and 49th Fighter Group) *7*
Col. David L. Hill (AVG and 23rd Fighter Group) *13.25*
Col. Bruce K. Holloway (23rd Fighter Group) *13*
Lt. Col. George Kiser (17th Pursuit Squadron and 49th Fighter Group) *9*
Lt. John D. Landers (49th Fighter Group) *6*
Lt. James W. Little (23rd Fighter Group) *7*
Capt. John D. Lombard (51st and 23rd Fighter Groups) *7*
Maj. Lyman Middleditch (57th Fighter Group) *5*
Col. William H. Momyer (33rd Fighter Group) *8*
Capt. James B. Morehead (17th Pursuit Squadron and 49th Fighter Group) *7*
Capt. Robert J. Overcash (57th Fighter Group) *5*
Lt. MacArthur Powers (324th Fighter Group) *5*
Capt. Roger C. Pryor (23rd Fighter Group) *5*
Maj. William Reed (AVG; 3rd Chinese American Composite Wing) *3 in AVG; 6 in 3CACW*
Lt. Andrew J. Reynolds (17th Pursuit Squadron and 49th Fighter Group) *9.33*
Capt. Elmer Richardson (23rd Fighter Group) *8*
Col. Robert L. Scott Jr. (23rd Fighter Group) *13*
Capt. Lucien Shuler (18th Fighter Group) *7*
Capt. Ralph G. Taylor (325th Fighter Group) *6*
Col. C. D. Vincent (23rd Fighter Group) *6*
Lt. Col. Boyd D. Wagner (24th Pursuit Group) *5*
Capt. Walter B. Walker Jr. (325th Fighter Group) *5*
Maj. Robert Westbrook (18th Fighter Group) *7*
Capt. W. M. Whaedon (18th Fighter Group) *7*
Maj. Roy Whittaker (57th Fighter Group) *7*

Percy R. Bartelt (AVG) *5*
William E. Bartling (AVG) *5*
Charles R. Bond (AVG) *7*
George Burgard (AVG) *10*
Robert Hedman (AVG) *6*
Kenneth A. Jernstedt (AVG) *5 (revised tally)*
Frank Lawlor (AVG) *7*
Robert L. Little (AVG) *10*
William D. McGarry (AVG) *8*
Robert H. Neale (AVG) *13*
John V. K. Newkirk (AVG) *7*
Charles Older (AVG) *10*
Ed Overend (AVG) *5*
Robert W. Prescott (AVG) *5.50*
Ed Rector (AVG) *6.75*
John R. Rossi (AVG) *6.25*
Robert J. Sandell (AVG) *5*
Robert H. Smith (AVG) *5*
Robert T. Smith (AVG) *9*

Flight Officer Andrew Barr (RAAF 3 Sqdn) *11*
Maj. Andrew C. Bosman (4 and 2 Sqdns, SAAF) *8*
Flight Officer Neville Bowker (RAF 112 Sqdn) *8*
Group Captain Clive R. Caldwell (Australian in RAF) *20.50*
Wing Commander Billy Drake (RAF) *14 or 15*
Squadron Leader Neville Duke (RAF) *5*
Flight Officer G. B. Fiskin (RNZAF 15 Sqdn) *5*
Squadron Leader R. H. Gibbes (RAAF 3 Sqdn) *10.50*
Maj. D. W. Golding (SAAF 4 Sqdn) *9*
Squadron Leader G. P. H. Newton *5*
Wing Commander A. C. Rawlinson (Australian in N. Africa) *5*
Maj. Eric Saville (SAAF 2 Sqdn; RAF 112 Sqdn) *8*
Flight Leader John L. Waddy (Australian in RAF) *12.50*
Flight Leader R. J. C. Whittle (Australian in N. Africa; RAF 250 Sqdn) *11.50*
Senior Lt. Nicolai Kuynetzov (Soviet 72nd Fighter Air Regiment) *15*
Guards Maj. Peter Adreivich Pilyutov (USSR) *5*
Senior Lt. Stepan Grigorievich Ridney (USSR) *10*
Maj. Kun Tan (China) *5*
Capt. Hsi-Lan Tsang (China) *6*
Lt. Kuang-Fu Wang (China) *7.50*

This list represents aces who achieved that status entirely with P-40 victories; some other aces not listed here had a portion of their victories in P-40s. Some of the aces on this list also scored additional victories in other types of aircraft. Some victories were shared by more than two pilots, and subsequent lists occasionally vary slightly over fractionalization. A few tallies may include unconfirmed victories as well. The global use of P-40s makes chronicling all activities of its many pilots difficult; more P-40 aces may yet surface. Sources of information on P-40 aces include: *Aces High,* by Robert E. Cunningham (General Dynamics); *Aces of the Southwest Pacific,* by Gene B. Stafford (Squadron/Signal); *American Combat Planes,* by Ray Wagner (Doubleday); *Checkertail Clan,* by Ernest R. McDowell and William N. Hess (Arco); *Fighters over the Desert,* by Christopher Shores and Hans Ring (Arco); *Ninth Air Force Story,* by Kenn C. Rust (Historical Aviation Album); *The P-40 Kittyhawk,* by Ernest R. McDowell (Arco); and *Twelfth Air Force Story,* by Kenn C. Rust (Historical Aviation Album). Research by Barrett Tillman, with reference to Frank Olynyk, is gratefully acknowledged.

End Notes

1. George W. Gray, *Frontiers of Flight—The Story of NACA Research,* Alfred A. Knopf: New York, 1948.
2. James R. Hansen, *Engineer in Charge—A History of the Langley Aeronautical Laboratory, 1917-1958,* NASA: Washington, D.C., 1987.
3. Ibid.
4. Peter M. Bowers, *Curtiss Aircraft, 1907–1947,* Putnam: London, 1979.
5. Benjamin S. Kelsey, *The Dragon's Teeth? The Creation of United States Air Power for World War II,* Smithsonian Institution Press: Washington, D.C., 1982.
6. Ibid.
7. Ibid.
8. Peter M. Bowers, *Curtiss Aircraft, 1907–1947,* Putnam: London, 1979.
9. Ibid.
10. Paraphrased coded radiogram from LEE (probably Col. Raymond E. Lee, acting senior U.S. military attaché in Lo024ndon) to the Secretary of War, et al., Subject (not delineated on document): Comparison of P-40 with Spitfire II and Hurricane II, 23 December 1940.
11. Ibid.
12. Ibid.
13. Message, GHQ SWPA (General MacArthur) to CG AAF (General Arnold), Subject (not delineated on memo): Combat comparisons of P-40, P-39, and "0" fighters, 14 May 1942.
14. Ibid.
15. Ibid.
16. "History of the 4146th AAF BU's (Dover, Del.) Rocket Development Program as Conducted for the Army Air Forces," circa 1946 (original filed at Air Force Historical Research Agency, Maxwell AFB, Alabama).
17. Letter, 1Lt. John M. Colmant, Ordnance, to Capt. William Black, Subj: "Initial Operational Use of Rocket Projectiles - March 4, 1944. Target - Air Field at Hainan Island, China", 7 March 1944.
18. Message, CG, 14th Air Force, Kunming (Gen. Chennault) to Gen. Arnold, Subj: [not delineated on message] Fighter Rocket Attack Summary, 24 March 1944.
19. "Fighter Ski Development Including P-36, P-40, P-38, P-51, P-47, and P-63", AAF Technical Report No. 5293, AAF HQ Air Technical Service Command, circa 1946.
20. Ibid.
21. Henry C. Fadden, Curtiss-Wright Corp., to N. L. Kearney, Curtiss-Wright Corp., Communication No. 4227, from HQ, Air Service Command, Fifth Air Force, 20 March 1943.
22. Ibid.
23. Ibid.
24. Ibid.
25. Ibid.
26. Ibid.
27. "Installation of 3 Belly Tanks on P-40," HQ 49th Fighter Group, AAF, 1 September 1944.
28. Ibid.
29. "Final Report on Test of Operational Suitability of P-40N-1 Airplane," Proof Department, AAF Proving Ground Command, Eglin Field, Florida, 7 June 1943.
30. Ibid.
31. Ibid.
32. Ibid.
33. Ibid.
34. Letter, 45th Fighter Squadron CO to 15th Fighter Group CO, et al., Subj: "Bomb Loads and Characteristics of the P-40N-5-CU and P-40K-1 Airplanes," 24 February 1944.
35. Ibid.
36. Ibid.
37. Ibid.
38. Ibid.
39. Ibid.
40. Includes 113 P-38s built by Convair/Nashville, Tennessee, in 1945.
41. Does not include 500 A-36s.
42. *Army Air Forces Statistical Digest—World War II,* Office of Statistical Control, HQ, Army Air Forces, December 1945.
43. Irving Brinton Holley, Jr., *United States Army in World War II—Special Studies—Buying Aircraft: Materiel Procurement for the Army Air Forces,* Center for Military History, United States Army: Washington, D.C., 1989.
44. Kit C. Carter and Robert Mueller, compilers, *Combat Chronology, 1941–1945, U.S. Army Air Forces in World War II,* Center for Air Force History: Washington, D.C., 1991.
45. Conversation, author with Col. Francis Gabreski, USAF (Ret.), August 1995.
46. Kit C. Carter and Robert Mueller, compilers, *Combat Chronology, 1941–1945, U.S. Army Air Forces in World War II,* Center for Air Force History: Washington, D.C., 1991.
47. *Army Air Forces Statistical Digest—World War II,* Office of Statistical Control, HQ, Army Air Forces, December 1945.
48. Kit C. Carter and Robert Mueller, compilers, *Combat Chronology, 1941–1945, U.S. Army Air Forces in World War II,* Center for Air Force History: Washington, D.C., 1991.
49. *Army Air Forces Statistical Digest—World War II,* Office of Statistical Control, HQ, Army Air Forces, December 1945.
50. Medical History, 23rd Fighter Group, 1 October 1944–1 March 1945 (filed at Air Force Historical Research Agency).
51. Kit C. Carter and Robert Mueller, compilers, *Combat Chronology, 1941–1945, U.S. Army Air Forces in World War II,* Center for Air Force History: Washington, D.C., 1991.
52. Ibid.
53. *Army Air Forces Statistical Digest—World War II,* Office of Statistical Control, HQ, Army Air Forces, December 1945.
54. Kit C. Carter and Robert Mueller, compilers, *Combat Chronology, 1941–1945, U.S. Army Air Forces in World War II,* Center for Air Force History: Washington, D.C., 1991.
55. Ibid.
56. Ibid.
57. Ibid.
58. Ibid.
59. Ibid.
60. Kenn C. Rust, *Twelfth Air Force Story,* Historical Aviation Album: Temple City, California, 1975.
61. Ann Cooper, "A Curtiss P-40N highlights World War II action over the South Pacific in Jack Fellows' painting," *Aviation History,* November 1995, (Pp. 66-67).
62. Ibid.

63. Rene J. Francillon, *Japanese Aircraft of the Pacific War,* Naval Institute Press: Annapolis, Maryland, 1988.
64. Kit C. Carter and Robert Mueller, compilers, *Combat Chronology, 1941–1945, U.S. Army Air Forces in World War II,* Center for Air Force History: Washington, D.C., 1991.
65. Ibid.
66. Eduard Mark, *Aerial Interdiction in Three Wars,* Center for Air Force History, Washington, D.C., 1994.
67. Kit C. Carter and Robert Mueller, compilers, *Combat Chronology, 1941–1945, U.S. Army Air Forces in World War II,* Center for Air Force History: Washington, D.C., 1991.
68. Alfred M. Beck, chief editor; Bernard C. Nalty, John F. Shiner, George M. Watson, *With Courage: The U.S. Army Air Forces in World War II,* Air Force History and Museums Program: Washington, D.C., 1994.
69. Wesley Frank Craven and James Lea Cate, editors, *The Army Air Forces in World War II,* ,Vol. Five, Imprint by the Office of Air Force History: Washington, D.C., 1983.
70. Kit C. Carter and Robert Mueller, compilers, *Combat Chronology, 1941–1945, U.S. Army Air Forces in World War II,* Center for Air Force History: Washington, D.C., 1991.
71. *Army Air Forces Statistical Digest—World War II,* Office of Statistical Control, HQ, Army Air Forces, December 1945.
72. Special Study, "American Volunteer Group", circa 1942, Air Force Historical Research Agency collection, Maxwell AFB, Alabama.
73. Maurer Maurer, *Aviation in the U.S. Army, 1919-1939,* Office of Air Force History, Washington, D.C., 1987.
74. Ibid.
75. Special Study, "American Volunteer Group", circa 1942, Air Force Historical Research Agency collection, Maxwell AFB, Alabama.
76. Herbert Weaver (Wesley Frank Craven and James Lea Cate, editors), *The Army Air Forces in World War II, Vol. I,* reprinted by the Office of Air Force History: Washington, D.C., 1983.
77. Special Study, "American Volunteer Group", circa 1942, Air Force Historical Research Agency collection, Maxwell AFB, Alabama.
78. Ibid.
79. Report, "Three Years With the 23rd," by Office of the Historical Officer, 23rd Fighter Group, 31 May 1945.
80. Herbert Weaver (Wesley Frank Craven and James Lea Cate, editors), *The Army Air Forces in World War II, Vol. I,* reprinted by the Office of Air Force History: Washington, D.C., 1983.
81. Ibid.
82. Special Study, "American Volunteer Group", circa 1942, Air Force Historical Research Agency collection, Maxwell AFB, Alabama.
83. Ibid.
84. Ibid.
85. Ibid.
86. Ibid.
87. Ibid.
88. Ibid.
89. "Fighter Tactics of the A.V.G.," Included under cover letter, Subj: Information on Tactics of A.V.G., from HQ Army Air Forces, A. W. Brock, Jr., Colonel, GSC, Director of Intelligence Service, 27 August 1942.
90. Ibid.
91. Headquarters U.S. Air Forces in India—Tenth U.S. Air Force, "Informal report on A.V.G. Activities and Experiences," by C. W. Sawyer, Robert Layher, and Robert Smith, To: All Units, 10th Air Force, Delhi, India, 2 May 1942.
92. Ibid.
93. Ibid.
94. Ibid.
95. Ibid.
96. Ibid.
97. Ibid.
98. 26th Ferrying Wing, Air Transport Command, Accra, B.W. Africa, "Interrogation of AVG Pilots," 11 July 1942, by Capt. Harry R. Turkel, S-2, 26th Ferrying Wing.
99. Notes on Interview with George L. Paxton, A.V.G. Pilot, 8/25/42," Included under cover letter, Subj: Information on Tactics of A.V.G., from HQ Army Air Forces, A. W. Brock, Jr., Colonel, GSC, Director of Intelligence Service, 27 August 1942.
100. Ibid.
101. Combat Report—Attack Against Enemy Aircraft—Flight Leader Greene," Included under cover letter, Subject: Information on Tactics of A.V.G., from HQ Army Air Forces, A.W. Brock, Jr., Colonel, GSC, Director of Intelligence Service, August 27, 1942.
102. Ibid.
103. Low-Flying Attack by Allied Aircraft," Included under cover letter, Subj: Information on Tactics of A.V.G., from HQ Army Air Forces, A. W. Brock, Jr., Colonel, GSC, Director of Intelligence Service, 27 August 1942.
104. Interview with W. W. Pentecost, 4/28/42," Included under cover letter, Subj: Information on Tactics of A.V.G., from HQ Army Air Forces, A. W. Brock, Jr., Colonel, GSC, Director of Intelligence Service, 27 August 1942.
105. Ibid.
106. Ibid.
107. Interview with Mr. Frank G. Metasavage, A.V.G. Mechanic, 8/5/42," Included under cover letter, Subj: Information on Tactics of A.V.G., from HQ Army Air Forces, A. W. Brock, Jr., Colonel, GSC, Director of Intelligence Service, 27 August 1942.
108. Letter, 23rd Fighter Group Office of the Commanding Officer, to Commanding Officer, 14th Air Service Command, 13 September 1943, Subj: Replacement of Aircraft.
109. Dr. Frank Olynyk, "AVG and USAAF CBI Credits for Destruction of Enemy Aircraft," privately published in 1986. (This is regarded by some fighter aces experts as the definitive tally of AVG victories; varying totals have been published in a variety of sources ever since the war.)
110. History, 332nd Fighter Group, Air Force Historical Research Agency, Maxwell AFB, Alabama.
111. Ibid.
112. Ibid.
113. Robert A. Rose, DDS, *Lonely Eagles—The Story of America's Black Air Force in World War II,* Tuskegee Airmen Inc., Los Angeles Chapter: Los Angeles, Calif., 1976.
114. Ibid.
115. Ibid.
116. Ibid.
117. Ibid.
118. Report, "Operations of the 99th Fighter Squadron Compared with Other P-40 Squadrons in MTO, 3 July 1943—31 January 1944," (SC-SP-496), by Statistical Control Division, Office of Management Control, 30 March 1944.
119. Ibid.
120. Ibid.
121. Alan L. Gropman, *The Air Force Integrates, 1945–1964,* Office of Air Force History: Washington, D.C., 1978.
122. "Report of the 17th Pursuit Squadron (Provisional) Activity in Java," circa Jan-Feb 1942, retained by the Air Force Historical Research Agency, Maxwell AFB, Alabama.
123. Ibid.
124. Ibid.
125. Ibid.

126. Rene J. Francillon, *Japanese Aircraft of the Pacific War,* Naval Institute Press: Annapolis, Maryland, 1988.
127. "Report of the 17th Pursuit Squadron (Provisional) Activity in Java," circa Jan-Feb 1942, retained by the Air Force Historical Research Agency, Maxwell AFB, Alabama.
128. Ibid.
129. W. F. Craven and J. L. Cate, editors, *The Army Air Forces in World War II,* Vol. I, "Plans & Early Operations—January 1939 to August 1942", Office of Air Force History: Washington, D.C., 1983.
130. "Report of the 17th Pursuit Squadron (Provisional) Activity in Java," circa Jan-Feb 1942, retained by the Air Force Historical Research Agency, Maxwell AFB, Alabama.
131. Ibid.
132. Ibid.
133. Ibid.
134. "Japanese Warhawk!" by Yasushi Ushijima as translated by Osamu Tagaya, *American Aviation Historical Society Journal,* Volume 20, Number 2, Summer 1975.
135. W. F. Craven and J. L. Cate, editors, *The Army Air Forces in World War II,* Vol. IV, "The Pacific: Guadalcanal to Saipan—August 1942 to July 1944", Office of Air Force History: Washington, D.C., 1983.
136. "Comparison of Effectiveness of the Chinese Air Force (P-40s) and Selected 14th AF Fighter Units of Comparable Strength (For Period 1 July to 30 Sept. 1944), by 24 SCU (Statistical Control Unit), 27 October 1944.
137. Ibid.
138. Ibid.
139. W. F. Craven and J. L. Cate, editors, *The Army Air Forces in World War II,* Vol. IV, "The Pacific: Guadalcanal to Saipan—August 1942 to July 1944," Office of Air Force History: Washington, D.C., 1983.
140. "'Snake Dance' Strafing in China,' *Informational Intelligence Summary* No. 44-21, 10 July 1944, Office of the Assistant Chief of Air Staff, Intelligence: Washington, D.C.
141. 49th Fighter Group, "Group Historical Records (September 1944)," dated 27 November 1944.
142. Vincent Orange, *Coningham—A Biography of Air Marshal Sir Arthur Coningham,* Center for Air Force History: Washington, D.C., 1992.
143. Eduard Mark, *Aerial Interdiction in Three Wars,* Center for Air Force History: Washington, D.C., 1994.
144. Vincent Orange, *Coningham —A Biography of Air Marshal Sir Arthur Coningham,* Center for Air Force History: Washington, D.C., 1992.
145. Ibid.
146. Ibid.
147. Report, Military Intelligence Division, War Department General Staff, to Assistant Chief of Staff, G-2, "Final Report of Lt. W. W. Momyer, Air Corps, on trip to Egypt," 6 October 1941.
148. Ibid.
149. Ibid.
150. Ibid.
151. "Air Phase of the North African Invasion," U.S. Air Force Historical Study No. 105, Assistant Chief of Air Staff, Intelligence, Historical Division, 1942.
152. Ibid.
153. Inter-Office Memorandum, Curtiss-Wright Corp., Subj: "Pilots Comments and Suggestions," 9 February 1943.
154. Inter-Office Memorandum, Curtiss-Wright Corp., Subj: "Enemy Aircraft—Messerschmitt 109G-2," 9 February 1943.
155. After-action report, Mission No. 62, 30 April 1943, by Capt. Barney E. Turner, 86th Fighter Squadron.
156. Interview, author with Maj Gen John R. Alison, USAF (Ret.), August 1996.
157. Ibid.
158. Ibid.
159. "Pearl Harbor and Beyond," John L. Frisbee, *Air Force Magazine,* May 1993.
160. Interview, author with Col. Ken Glassburn, USAF (Ret.), March 1998.
161. Ibid.
162. Ibid.
163. Caption to photograph of F/Lt. M. T. Vanderpump receiving DFC (from USAF archives, Maxwell AFB, Alabama).
164. Ibid.
165. Ibid.
166. Interview, author with Gene Chase, March 1998.
167. John Chapman and Geoff Goodall, *Warbirds Worldwide Directory,* Mansfield, England, 1989.
168. Peter M. Bowers, *Curtiss Aircraft, 1907–1947,* Putnam: London, 1979.
169. Frank B. Mormillo, "This P-40 Has Credit for WWII Enemy Shootdown," *Pacific Flyer,* May 1988.
170. Peter M. Bowers, *Curtiss Aircraft, 1907–1947,* Putnam: London, 1979.
171. Ernest R. McDowell, *The P-40 Kittyhawk,* Arco Publishing: New York, N.Y., 1968.
172. Ibid.
173. Ibid.
174. From notes and publications in the collection of Middle East scholar Dr. Gary Leiser.

Glossary

AAF	Army Air Forces
AF	Air Force or Air Forces
CAF	Chinese Air Force
CATF	China Air Task Force
CBI	China-Burma-India Theater of Operations
FB	Fighter-Bomber
FEAF	Far East Air Force
HE	High Explosive (bomb)
HVAR	High Velocity Aircraft Rocket
Kittybomber	RAF Kittyhawk adapted for bombing missions in North Africa
MAAF	Mediterranean Allied Air Forces
MTO	Mediterranean Theater of Operations
NAAF	Northwest African Air Forces
NATAF	Northwest African Tactical Air Force
NASAF	Northwest African Strategic Air Force
NEI	Netherlands East Indies
RAF	Royal Air Force
RP-40	The use of the prefix letter "R" during the era of the P-40 indicated an aircraft no longer suited to its primary mission. Older, non-combat-worthy P-40s were so designated.
USAAF	United States Army Air Forces
WDAF	Western Desert Air Force (in Africa)
ZI	Zone of the Interior (continental United States)

Index